LSP #1

Letters to a soul

LETTERS TO A SOUL
Hubert van Zeller

Sheed and Ward . London

To the soul to whom they were written

LETTER 1

Dear X,

You have asked me to tell you where I think you have made mistakes in the past and how to avoid making the same mistakes in the future. Since the request has come from you I can be frank in what I write. You for your part will have to be humble. You do not have to take what advice I give. You do not have to agree with my opinions. All you have to do is to see whether or not the things I write apply. If they don't apply, forget them. In a correspondence of this sort there are two mistakes to be avoided: one by you and one by me. I mean it would be stretching the purpose of what I suppose we must call 'direction' if you were to feel yourself cramped by what I suggest. The point of spiritual direction is to bring about greater freedom, not greater constraint. What I shall try to do is to help you to make decisions. I do not exist as a prop, as someone who conveniently makes decisions for you. Direction can all too easily limit freewill instead of providing a more Godward, and therefore a greater, range for its exercise. So much for the possible mistake at the receiving end. At the delivering end, at my end, the mistake to be avoided is softening the principle to suit the sensibilities—to make things sound easier than they are meant to be.

You mention your discouragement and the sense of failure. You say you are trying to resist the obvious temptation to be discontented and bitter, and that everything you attempt only increases your feeling of inadequacy. But isn't this because you expected a certain kind of success and have not found it? Wouldn't it be better to accept your limitations and be content within them? It is an art in life to put up with being second best. I don't mean that we must make compromises with our weaknesses, but I do mean that we have to admit we are mediocrities. To accept the role we have to play, even if it's a small part when we have the talent to play the more important and successful one, is not to invite failure or frustration. It is to submit to the condition of life which God has planned for us. Once we have made this submission—which is not a lowering of an ideal but on the contrary, because it essentially involves humility, is a raising of the ideal of serving God in truth— we are less disappointed at the evidence of our inadequacy. Accepting our mediocrity, while all the time trying to make the most of our opportunity, not only brings a certain peace but is what the parable of the talents is all about. So long as we don't bury the insignificant talent, and put the blame on God for its insignificance, we can go on trading with it as effectively as the more talented. Notice how our Lord commends not the man with the ten or the man with the five talents but the man with the few: 'Because you have been faithful with the *few*'—which were all I gave you, is the implication—'I will turn them into many'. It will mark a great step forward when you face the fact that you are not the hero or the saint or the leader that you thought you were. You will then be able to get on with the business of being the person you actually are. And this will mean less discontent.

So what it all amounts to—at least this is the impression I get though I may be wrong—is that you are trying too hard. You are wanting to push God's will about. You are setting the pace instead of letting God set it. Try not to struggle and kick so violently and you may find more peace. It's no good fighting the life God gives you. It only makes it worse. The life you have

8

got, like the personality you have got, may not be the one you would have chosen. It may not be the best life (or the best personality), but it is the best one for you, or God would have given you another one. Don't hit out at it so much. Do you fish ever, I forget? Well, a fish at the end of a line wriggles and makes a great fuss. It threshes about trying to get off the hook. But when you have landed it and it is lying on the grass, still alive, it knows there's no point in fighting any more. It accepts the inevitable and what is left to it of life is peace. A twitch every now and then, by way of mild protest before the end, but desperation no longer. I don't say you are near the end but I do say that hitting out at the position you happen to be in is a mistake.

More and more as I get older I come to see the wisdom of St Francis of Sales where he says *Là où Dieu nous a semés il faut savoir fleurir*. But it takes a lot of learning. St Paul taught the same thing: 'I have learned in whatsoever state I am to be content therewith.' Don't you think contentment is about as much as we can hope for? I don't think we can expect happiness—not as an abiding condition any-way—so to be reasonably contented with what we have salvaged from the flotsam and jetsam of life is a good for which we should be grateful. All it needs is to trust in God's providence, and to work on the virtue of hope. The important thing is to believe that God has made you what you are, has put you in a particular century in which to do that work. Don't try to break out of the ring of God's providence. By accepting its boundaries you arrive, paradoxically, at freedom. By banging your head against them you don't get rid of them and you only give yourself a headache.

Yours, Dom

Dear X,

After writing my last letter I felt you might mis-understand a part of it. This is what has happened exactly. When you say 'I'm damned if I should accept second best' it shows you have taken one or two re-marks out of their context. Before blowing up about this or that sentence of mine I wish you would read the whole letter. (Very few people do this, and I find most of my correspondents assume from the start that they know what I am going to say and accordingly pay little attention to what in fact I do say.)

Let me get this straight about 'accepting second best'. Isn't most of life a matter of accepting second best—when deprived by necessity of what one thinks is *the* best? And aren't most of the mistakes we make brought about by stretching out to a best which we are never meant to have? We have to 'know our place', and not to move 'above our station'. Lucifer did not know his place—you would have thought the station of an archangel would have been good enough —and his last recorded words were 'I will not serve'. Nor did Adam know his place but wanted a knowl-edge which was no business of his. It has been the same all the way down the line of failed vocation: Saul, Judas, Henry Tudor. None of them was con-tent to stay in the second best place, so either rebelled or deserted—or both. The saints accepted whatever place they were put in and did not question the pro-vidence of God. To fight our place in life is to fight life itself so, logically, to fight God. In one way or another everyone has to accept second best for him-self. The happily married man takes second place to his family, the happily professed religious takes second place to his community. The artist, the writer, the composer, the actor: each has to sublimate himself in order to express himself. In gospel terms the seed has to die if it is to come to harvest, the man has to lose his life if he is to find it. Your objection to the second best shows how you have mistaken perfectionism for perfection.

I haven't finished with this subject yet because while pausing for breath (and letting the typewriter cool) I came across a card I had been looking for and thought I had lost. On it is printed a litany composed by Cardinal Merry del Val which sums up what I have been trying to tell you. The whole litany is worth studying—and I'll copy it out if you want to read it—but the invocations which bear out the above doctrine about the willingness to take a back seat are these (each one is followed by the words 'Jesus, grant me the grace to desire it'): 'That others may be thought more of than I . . . that in the opinion of the world, others may increase and I may decrease . . . that others may be chosen and I set aside . . . that others may be praised and I unnoticed . . . that others may be preferred to me in everything . . . that others become holier than I, provided that I may become as holy as I should.' It is this last sentence that should be especially noticed. If good people, people who are trying to become saints, really took that part of the litany to heart they would see how misconceived is the approach which wants to rush it and climb to the top.

Anyway that is quite enough for today but if you want me to be more specific you have only to ask.

Yours,
Dom

Dear X,

Since you say in your letter that you are feeling sorry for yourself while you are writing I suggest that, without putting it into words, you know the answer to your problem. 'I have given God so much more' is your complaint, 'than he has given me. I accepted the grace of conversion from sin and worldliness and all the old life, and what have I got in return? Nothing but loneliness, alienation, non-comprehension.' Well, if religion is essentially the life of faith, what do you expect? You see only what you have given to God, not what he has given to you. When you accepted the grace of conversion you didn't haggle. You didn't say 'I'll alter my way of life provided you make it worth my while. In return for the renunciations it is only fair to expect something back.' You cannot strike a bargain with God. 'Seek first the kingdom of God' and to seek first the privileges of belonging to that kingdom is to get the order wrong. If you are deprived of the 'consolations of religion' you should remember that it was religion and not consolation that was the object of your conversion. You have not chosen the good and rejected the bad because the good is beautiful and the bad is ugly; you do not pray because prayer attracted you and sin disgusted you; you have not given yourself to the service of God for what you can get out of it but for what you can give to it. Your faith led to your conversion, and now your conversion is leading you on in the way of faith.

You would feel far less lonely if you forgot about how you would act if you were God—handing out compensations and spiritual sweetness to your friends in recognition of their commitment to your service—

and concentrated on the fuller and more interior implications of faith. Always in the service of God there is this confrontation of faith and feeling. We acknowledge the necessity of faith, but we want faith to be accompanied by feeling. We think feeling must confirm faith, but if faith is what it is meant to be it is more often confirmed by the withdrawal of feeling. Religious sentiment is good enough as far as it goes, and is a great help in the beginning, but it can be misleading. It can be ranked above trust. It can be made the touchstone of prayer, charity, service and everything connected with religion. The compensations and consolations of religion need to be supported by the will, and if they are not they may eventually take over from the will. Faith and trust reside in the will, compensation and consolation are matter for the emotions.

The will is the faculty which chooses and goes on choosing. It was the will which was at work when you decided to give up one way of life and take on another. Your conversion was not an emotional experience—though the emotions were mixed up in it—but an act of deliberate response of your whole self to God's grace. No strings attached. Now that you have fully responded, and now that God has accepted your response, you are very naturally, but mistakenly, wanting something to show for what has taken place between you and God. You are wanting him to bless your new life by providing you with a new zest for the new life. But if he did, where would be the faith? He is blessing it all right but at a level where feeling is not the final arbiter.

If you were to munch on a mouthful of honey you would taste both too much of it and not enough. To taste honey properly you have to put something underneath it—something ordinary and solid and dull like a piece of bread or toast. The service of God, which is a day-to-day fidelity, is for the most part ordinary and dull. But it is more solid than the sweetness which it supports and sometimes enjoys. So the moral of all this is 'look after the bread and the honey can look after itself'. Religion is neither a means of providing satisfaction nor a poultice applied to an injury. It is yielding. It is reaping too, but this aspect is best left to God. Yielding is a matter of the will, of faith, of trust: these are the important things. Reaping is important too, but we are apt to mistake enjoyment for it.

Yours,
Dom

LETTER 4

Dear X,

When we met the other day I was glad to find you had not been put off by the tone of attack in my letters, and that on your own initiative you took up the point I was trying to make in my last one. You said you could see the logic of the faith-and-feeling argument, and that you were getting used to the idea of having to do without spiritual consolations. Having to do without human consolations, you said, was what was now bothering you. 'I don't see myself spending the rest of my life without the kind of relationships which kept me going before my conversion.' (I know it is maddening to be quoted, but since this was uppermost in your mind at the time and you mentioned it more than once you will agree that it's something which should be gone into. Also it comes under the heading of compensations already discussed, though this time the compensations you are thinking about are natural and human, not spiritual and devotional.)

First of all you obviously cannot spend the rest of your life without human relationships of any kind. God certainly does not ask this of you, and I doubt if he asks it even of the saints. So the field narrows itself to those associations which are for you occasions of sin. (I said at this point in the conversation, if you remember, 'You mean sex?' and you answered 'Well, let's call it human relationship'.) Where occasions of sin are concerned, you know the course to be followed. The classification 'necessary' and 'unnecessary' occasions gives viable direction here: the situations forced upon you by circumstances or duty are warnings rather than inevitable opportunities, but not be taken advantage of and used as an excuse to commit sin; the situations you create for yourself are your own responsibility, and you have only yourself to blame if you use them sinfully. So I am afraid those human relationships to which you refer as belonging to your pre-conversion period, and which presumably involved sin, will have to be dropped. And no new ones of the same kind can be risked. But do remember that this does not cut you off from forming close intimate friendships, even romantic attachments. Only wrong love is wrong. Your pre-conversion experience should give you your standards of judgment in these things. Just because what is generally called an 'affair' is ruled out—and the term supposes what I in my rough simple way allude to as sex—you are not expected to trample on your affections or turn away the moment anyone attracts you. From now onwards it will be largely a question of training yourself in love, training yourself to love safely and not harmfully, truly and not superficially.

If you reply to this letter by telling me I am asking you to get rid of some of your nearest friends just because they have been occasions of sin once or twice, I can save you the trouble of putting the objection. All I am asking you to do is what God is asking you to do, which is to take a straight look at your relationships—past, present, and those that come up in the future—as they are in his sight. Take a relationship into the presence of God and you will know at once whether it is predominantly an occasion of sin and to be renounced or an occasion of gratitude to God and to be developed. Apply this test and let me know how it works.

Yours,
Dom

Dear X,

So after applying the test I suggested you are still doubtful. To be doubtful may be a good sign. At least it shows you want to do what is right. As far as conduct goes, doubt can be a good safeguard—just as giving oneself the benefit of the doubt can destroy the safeguards. Perhaps it would clarify the principle I outlined in my last letter if you brought it to bear upon each attachment separately, putting the association through a sort of sieve and examining as objectively as you can the impurities which have been left behind when the good stuff has got through. The question then to be asked is whether or not you have the courage to throw away what is left in the sieve. There must be few relationships which have to be ruthlessly broken if you are to stay in a state of grace. I imagine that quite a lot of yours could be salvaged. You will just have to see, but I'm firmly of the opinion that for a border-line relationship to be made safe there has to be a declaration of policy and principle and that the other person has to agree. Otherwise you are taking on more than your share of the load and will weaken under pressure.

Further on in your letter you say that by the time you are forty or forty-five you may be able to do without these dubious human relationships but that at your age and in the kind of world you live in you can hardly be expected to keep to the rules. 'It would mean I would have to be a hermit.' I don't agree at all. In the first place the notion that the pull towards worldliness, towards sin of any sort, slackens in middle age is a fallacy. You think that in your forties you won't get involved in people's lives and that your relationships will be smooth, untroubled by any sense of guilt, comfortably under control? Don't count on it. I am nearly seventy, and this has not been my experience at all. If anything, I think most temptations get stronger as one gets older, the only difference being that from past mistakes one acquires a certain presence of mind which allows one to pause where at an earlier age one would have plunged.

As to being forced by lack of doubtful relationships to live as a hermit in the world, this seems to me rather nonsense. To isolate yourself on the grounds that it is the only way of staying in a state of grace would be to alienate yourself. People do not become hermits out of fear or resentment against the world, and if they do they only become more afraid and more bitter and lonely. Also it is simply not true that the state of grace demands the closing of every avenue and putting a 'keep away' notice on the door. St Catherine of Siena wrote that there was no condition of life, apart from living in sin, which could not be brought to high perfection. No material circumstances, no surroundings or occupations, need get in the way of personal sanctification. So in order to have your love-life under control you do not have to leave the world. What you have to do is to see that your loves are not worldly and that your world is made up more of opportunities of loving God than of loving sin.

I can guess what your answer will be to all this so your next letter will find me sharpening my spears.

Yours,
Dom

LETTER 6

Dear X,

I know this sounds trite—something printed on a calendar issued by a firm of undertakers—but it is not the *when* or the *where* that matters but the *who* and the *how*. Your reply was broadly what I thought it would be, so in this letter I'll go on more or less from where I left off. But before you read on, please try to remember that every single soul is unique in God's sight and that general principles are accordingly helpful only to the degree that they affect the individual case. I am of course not talking now about those principles which are at the same time laws of God. I am talking of assumptions and conclusions arrived at either by accepted spiritual writers or by interpreting, speculatively it must be admitted, what spiritual writers have had to say. I mention this only to warn you that I may well be wrong in my reading the minds of those whose job it is to direct by means of the printed word. (As you see I am covering myself in case you come up with quotations from the Fathers which teach a different doctrine.)

Well then, you have four aspects of your problem —two of which I have said are unimportant compared with the other two—to consider: when, where, who, how. *When*, for all practical purposes, is now. Don't look into the remote future wondering if you will be able to keep up your present disposition of forming only those relationships which will do you good spiritually, or at all events will not do you spiritual harm. Also under the heading of 'when', don't live in a wistful memory of the past, wishing on the one hand you could resume some of the associations which you could not now go back to without being tortured with a sense of failure and guilt, or on the other hand loading your conscience with remorse. This is where you must take St Augustine's words to heart: 'Leave the past to the mercy of God, the future to the providence of God, and the present to the love of God'. So the *when* resolves itself into looking only at the present and trying to relate it practically and constructively to the love of God.

The question of *where* is, for the time being anyway, solved for you. You stay where you are, in the world as it was before your conversion and as it is now, making the best of your opportunities in serving God, however unpromising the environment. (This was what I meant in my last letter: the bit about St Catherine of Siena.)

The question of *who* is important precisely because no two 'whos' are alike and this is a highly individual problem. You have to take yourself as you are and not as you would wish you were (see the letter about fitting in to second place), and given your particular *ego* and *id* you have to work on the material in a way that does not break what you have got but instead builds up. We all think too subjectively anyway, so try to think of yourself objectively—as if you were someone else—and make your plans according to that *who*.

The question of *how* is clearly the most important of all, and my only advice is to answer it by means of prayer. In the light of prayer you will come to see the required measure of renunciation and, more positively, the way of going about the search for moral and spiritual perfection. The *how* amounts to asking the guidance of the Holy Spirit. But of course it is no good asking the Holy Spirit to guide you unless you mean to accept the guidance.　　Yours, Dom

LETTER 7

Dear X,

My letter seems to have been of no help at all, except that in a general way it made you review your position. Evidently it was the *where* which gave you pause, and brought up this idea of a possible vocation to the religious life. Feeling yourself to be a misfit in the world, you are perhaps looking to the religious state as a refuge. There is nothing wrong in this, and many good monks and nuns have begun their religious lives because they have wanted security, but a true vocation is seldom founded on the search for a convenient shelter. Nor is it founded on logical conclusion—'I am looking for perfection; perfection is impossible for my kind of temperament if I am to live in the world; I must therefore leave the world and become a religious'—but much more on a gradually increasing attraction. The life of prayer, community, submission to authority, renunciation of ownership, a planned daily service: these are things to which the soul called by God to enter religion feels gradually drawn. A religious vocation may call *from,* but more significantly it calls *to,* and the point you have to consider is whether your present feeling for the religious life is positive or negative, a desire for a fuller service of God or a desire to escape the temptations, responsibilities, cares and contingencies of the world. For all I know you may be called by God to take vows in an order, but before you apply anywhere for admission, ask yourself what really you are looking for and whether or not that something is attainable in your existing circumstances. You remember that couplet by James Thurber: 'All must learn before they die/what they are running from, and to, and why.' The best way to discover the will of God is to wait upon his grace as given you from day to day, and to trust that light will be given you if a change is to be made. *Leg dich krumm, so hilft dir Gott.* Where he sees detachment from selfwill he supplies the help you need to see what he wills. This of course supposes real detachment—readiness to accept his lead—and not the kind which masquerades as detachment which in fact is attachment to doing nothing.

A cargo ship in harbour which is listing to port or starboard cannot be loaded up to full capacity. Someone who is leaning to one side or another cannot be fully open to the knowledge of God's will. When we are in the dark about anything, the only way of getting light is to stand squarely before God and to ask that he may make the way more clear. Often it is in our own interest that he keeps us in the dark because were he to grant the light before we arrived at detachment there would be a good chance that we would turn away from it and go our own way and not his. If I seem to be doubtful about your having a religious vocation it is not because I lack confidence in you but because I think it is very easy for you to deceive yourself, and to deceive yourself at this stage might lead to a disappointment which would throw you back into a worldliness worse than the one you are trying, as I think, to escape. You are growing rapidly in the spirit, and at every stage of growth there is a desire to take shelter—as the psychiatrists would tell you—in the womb. Womb-vocations don't work. Security has to be sacrificed if it is to be secured. Jonah had to forget about the enclosure of the big fish. The catacombs would have been bad for the infant church if the faithful had wanted to stay in them for good.

Yours, Dom

LETTER 8

Dear X,

There is a line in Shaw's *Major Barbara* which you may remember. 'With every discovery' the tycoon Overshaft says, 'goes a sense of loss.' Not only do you miss the process of looking for what you have found but, more to the point here, you miss what you have had to give up on account of what you have found. Your conversion from worldliness and religious indifference was very real, a grace from God with which you co-operated, and the sense of loss which followed your discovery of God has left you with a void which, quite logically and commendably, you want to fill with more and more of God. This has led you to believe that you have a vocation. Perhaps you have. I'm no prophet. My only doubt is about the direction: direction from or direction to. Religious vocation supposes a movement towards. Life—all life but especially religious life—is progressive, is advance. Retreat is a holding operation, a rearguard action, and hardly life at all. I remember reading somewhere that the difference between the Sea of Galilee and the Dead Sea is that the one is alive because it pours out and that the other is sterile because it does not give. I am a bit afraid that in the religious life you might not pour out as you are doing now in the world which you despise so much, and that you might cease to give. The whole point of the religious life is giving. Not just, as I feel you think, giving up.

It may be that in the providence of God you may have to try the religious life before you arrive, one way or the other, at peace. I doubt in any case whether a complete follow-through vocation is granted to people who enter convents and monasteries. Perhaps those who have absolute confidence in God and a firm sense of mission are allowed to know before they take the habit that they will persevere on and on until they die. I think that for most people, and I know it was so with me, the vocational grace was a stage-by-stage affair. A soul gets a vocation to try the vocation. The grace is genuine enough but transitional. It is meant to tide the person over during a difficult interim period. Or the purpose may be to lay a ghost, to allow the person to return to the world without the haunting dread that God has never been given a chance.

If you decide to go ahead and give what you believe before God to be a call of grace a trial, then I would urge you to do it reasonably soon. If it is not a call of grace you will find this out and get it over, settling down without regrets. If it is a call of grace you should not delay your response. What often happens is that souls who possibly have a genuine vocation keep putting off the decision to enter until the attraction ceases to attract, and the vocation peters out. A religious vocation is a delicate thing and can be stifled either by waiting for greater certainty—and you can never be absolutely sure; it should anyway be a venture of faith—or by plunging into worldliness in the belief that a true vocation will show itself strong enough to survive all opposing influences. You do not plant a violet in poor soil, expose it to frost and deluge, trample on it and run a car over it, and then say 'If it is a good violet it will triumph over all tests.' Neither violets nor vocations are meant to be bludgeoned. I wish you well in this project of yours, whatever the outcome.

Yours,
Dom

LETTER 9

Dear X,

It is a long time since we have exchanged letters. I took it that you were not allowed to write letters while in the novitiate, and it seemed a mistake for me to write and thereby perhaps add to the conflicting ideas which I felt certain were troubling you. But now that you made the experiment of the religious life and are back in the world again I see no harm in picking up where we left off. One thing I beg of you: don't regret the experience—either to have entered the novitiate or to have left it. I am sure you have learned more about God, about people, about yourself, about the world and life generally than if you had not overridden my hesitations. Frankly I was against your trying your vocation because I feared you would be disappointed, if not disillusioned, but since you clearly went into it on the highest motive of wanting to follow the inspiration of the Holy Spirit, the time cannot have been wasted. And now it is the Holy Spirit, not your own self-will or unstable nature, who has taken you out of it.

The danger for you now, as I am sure you must know already, is to feel discouraged about religion in general and about yourself in particular. Don't let yourself be crushed by what looks like a failure. It is not a failure: it is an indication. It is not a retreat from grace but a means of learning more about grace: it is an indication of what God wants from you in the way of service. You gave him what you thought he wanted and he has shown you what in fact he does want. He tested you as he tested Abraham. It was not a mistake on Abraham's part that he offered Isaac: it was a sacrifice all right—with one detail not insisted on. You made your sacrifice when you left the world, and the detail of fulfilment in that particular vocation was not insisted on. And now Isaac has been given back to you and you must make the best of him. I remember so well how, when I came out after some months in a Carthusian novitiate, the sense of dismay robbed me of all religious purpose: I just wanted to sit with folded hands admitting to myself that I had proved myself to be a second-class citizen and that perfection was no longer open to me. I would have wasted far less time if I had worked on the graces given to those who are not Carthusians and not worried about missing the graces given to those who are. It is all a question of acting upon the graces which are given and not envying the graces which are not. The parable of the talents again.

Look at it this way. You are humiliated at not having persevered. But isn't this a perfectly natural expression of pride? Don't let it stop at a natural humiliation, at the thought of defeat where you expected triumph, but raise the whole experience to an act of further trust: trust in the providence of God which had planned something different, and trust in your ability to reach an even higher perfection than that which you would have reached if, mistakenly, you had continued in the religious life. I'll pray that you may learn the lesson of this.

Yours,
Dom

LETTER 10

Dear X,

Your letter interested me enormously. It also proved that you had deepened as the result of your time as a novice. I had feared you might be bitter but instead you seem to have acquired a certain humanity which was a little lacking before. And instead of feeling defeated (as I was after my Carthusian interlude) you seem to understand more clearly the kind of constructive role a serious catholic can play in the world. Your view of the world when you left it was jaundiced. You thought it had no other purpose than to seduce you. Now you seem to see there is something to be said for it after all—or anyway that there is much about it which can be saved and which wants to be saved. I'm sure the saints felt this about the world, and that it was this which prevented the whole lot fleeing into the desert. Certainly you learned far more when you were a novice than I did when I was, and are learning more now that you are not one. Only later, much later, did I come to see that though life in the world and life in religion are two very differing things, *life* is the same. This means that though different people follow different vocations according to their particular graces they share the same gift of living. The mere being alive is communicating, and I doubt if you would have come to acknowledge this if you hadn't chosen to be dead, as you hoped, to the world. To find life, we have to lose it, and when we have chosen to lose one kind of life we find we have discovered all life. Or at least we have come to understand the purpose of life. It is then that the purpose of life reveals itself as love. As nothing else but love.

The other night I was reading Turgenev and a paragraph in the book made me think of you. Now that I have had your letter I am reminded of it all the more. He speaks of a Russian nobleman who having moved from one European capital to another enjoying the raffish social life came back to his quiet country estate where he feared he would be bored stiff. Instead he became completely absorbed in 'the rural flow of life around him, in the streams and the woods and the farm animals'. Turgenev then goes on (and this is the point as regards you): 'he knew that in the other places where he had been the same life was seething and heaving and roaring *but it was the same life.*' (The italics of course are mine.) Whether you are in a religious house or a Hilton Hotel, your life is a part of everyone's life, and all life is God's. Your time in the novitiate gave you the disposition which could recognise this. You needed withdrawal from the world in order that you might appreciate the world. You needed first to value the interior monastic life—this was no difficulty because you appreciated it in theory before you tried it—and in turn the interior life gave you a perceptive power which was far more subtle and spiritual, enabling you to see the inwardness and reality underlying the 'seething, heaving, roaring' racket of the world. Now that you have got your perspectives—now that God has shown you how Christ managed to live in the world after the quiet of Nazareth—I think you will find it easier than after your conversion to adjust. I hope you will because otherwise you will go on resisting and looking for another escape. Don't try to escape, which would only lead to another disappointment and make you miserable, but try to accept.

Yours,
Dom

LETTER 11

Dear X,

I am glad you understand what I was trying to say in my last letter; I was afraid it might be obscure and badly put. But I am sure the point is important. We have to see life outside the monastery as being essentially the same as it is inside the monastery, but we come to see this more applicably when inside than when outside. Already from what you tell me the reaction, a perfectly natural one, has set in and with your memory of the light you received 'in there' you are dreading the darkened environment of 'out here'. I felt the same after my attempt at the Carthusian life: I felt the only truth lay within the contemplative enclosure, and that what I could remember of it was ebbing away fast. But this is a misconception. When God's light impresses its truth upon the soul the efficacy of the grace is not dependent upon the memory. This is so whether the experience of grace covers a period of time (as in a retreat or during a prolonged stay in a setting where recollection is practised) or whether it comes while the soul is employed in the actual exercise of prayer. You do not have to write down the points made clear to you in case you should happen to forget. This would make you the primary agent in whatever results God was planning to bring about. God himself is the cause of such knowledge as you may have picked up; he is also the inspiration, in bringing to your mind when the occasion presents itself, of such impulses on your part as may serve to further your perfection and his glory. I remember how, on leaving Parkminster forty years ago, I wasted no time in starting on a book which was to get on paper the supernatural wisdom I imagined I had acquired. (It was my first book and not at all a good one; happily it has been out of print for years.) The intention was more or less all right—mixed with vanity I'm afraid, in that I assumed I was wiser now and had a mission to broadcast my wisdom to the world—but what I had not understood was that God would be using his infused wisdom independently of my memory and in a way which I might never appreciate. The working of grace in the interior life is more often secret and incalculable than traceable and predictable. There is nothing strictly 'mystical' about this, in the sense that it comes under the heading of 'extraordinary phenomena'; any psychiatrist will tell you how the impressions registered consciously and subsequently forgotten may be stored up in the subconscious and brought to the surface if wanted later on.

The practical question for you is how to make the best use of the impressions (contemplative writers call them 'touches of the spirit') consciously received during your period of retirement from the world, always remembering, as I have said, that the deep penetration of these impressions of light and grace is what matters more. A very holy contemplative nun (Benedictine I'm glad to say) was talking to me two days ago, and I was telling her how much I had learned from her community, how the mass had meant more to me in Latin, how I hoped I might return to the convent for a longer stay. She listened and said 'Nothing must be wasted: we are given so much grace and always for a purpose: nothing must be wasted. Light must be used for others as well as for ourselves. Darkness too must be used. Everything we need is given. We must use and give back again: use and give *out* again.' This helped me a lot, and I hope it will help you. Grace is in circulation and we must put no obstacles to its passage. I'll have more to say about that in my next letter. This one is already long enough.

Yours,
Dom

Dear X,

I said I would go on with the same themes which threaded through my last letter, and since I have not heard of your reactions I might as well round off what has been in my mind and then you can tell me if what I have said has made things any clearer. After urging you to profit by all you have gone through in your search for a vocation I particularly want to add that the waste of interior grace can come about by one of two opposite ways of acting. Either we can scatter it, over-exposing it and not allowing it to take effect deep in the soul, or we can hoard it for ourselves without any intention of using it for the benefit of other people. When that nun spoke about not letting God's gifts go to waste I am sure she did not mean they were to be proclaimed from the housetops; what she meant was surely that we must learn from the Holy Spirit how to make our own decisions and how to help people who come to us. We can too easily mistake these touches or impressions of grace, interpreting them superficially when in fact their influence upon the soul is too deep for speculative or intellectual interpretation. I think you have been drawn by grace into an area which defies the ordinary assessments. I don't of course mean by this that you can afford to ignore the accepted standards or see revealed truths as merely symbols: all I mean is that you should guard against the slick application of a light the essential effect of which is too deep for you to appreciate.

The human mind is such that while it can get the grace right it can get the message wrong. King David is moved in prayer to build a house so he makes plans to get together bricks and mortar: the house God wanted was the house which was eventually to produce our Lord. You yourself were moved in prayer to give up all and follow Christ : the renunciation required of you was not a list of material things (tobacco, television, a car and so on) but the handing over of your whole self. The following of Christ was not, as you thought it was, the taking of the religious habit but the taking on of the religious commitment without qualification. This sort of thing is happening all the time and it must be enough to make the angels flap their wings with exasperation. The conclusion to be drawn is not to jump to conclusions. Let the conclusions have time to form themselves. So long as you allow them to be formed by God and not by human wisdom you cannot go far wrong. I know this sounds an old man's advice (which it is) but don't rush it. The voice of God, as Elijah discovered, is not in rush. It is not in the clash of rocks or in the storm of wind and rain. It is in the gentle breeze which is so gentle that it has to be listened for. All you young people are impatient of results. You want to turn things upside down to show your zeal for God's glory. You want to reform yourselves overnight and everyone else tomorrow morning. Incidentally that is why the changes in the church, mostly pushed along by youthful progressives, have been, because so rapid, so harsh and doubtfully inspired. Try not to show God what he wants. Let him show you.

Yours,
Dom

Dear X,

One good thing about you is that you never seem to resent my lecturing you on where I think you go wrong. Part of your trouble of course is that in addition to your being a would-be perfect follower of Christ you are a creative artist. You have tried since your conversion to live apart from your art. As a novice you were probably obliged by the timetable and the strictly convental setup to live apart from your art. Now the creative faculty cannot safely be corked up and left until a suitable opportunity arises for its exercise. People of talent, even if the talent amounts to no more than a goodish gift and has no pretension to genius, cannot live absolutely as people in their own right—cannot disassociate themselves from that part of themselves which is wanting to express itself. When talented people stop expressing themselves they stop thinking and become vegetables. Without their knowing it, and certainly not complaining about it (because to some it comes as a relief) the environment of their lives thins out, empties, diminishes. This I think happened to you when you discovered the life of grace, and thought that art, together with most forms of self-expression, must be unworthy of one who wanted to serve God with his whole heart and mind and soul. Deprived of the outlet which God had given you as a safety-valve while you lived as an unreflecting hedonist, you turned more and more into yourself and became very reflecting indeed. You asked yourself (and me) endless questions and either came up with no answers at all or else the wrong ones. Understandably you thought my direction too cautious and, since I had told you to go ahead with your own opinion if you felt mine to be wrong, you went ahead. You were right in doing this because you thought it was right. The fact is we really never know what God has in mind when he is drawing us to a particular way of life or to a particular place. All we can be sure of is that it is his love for us that is at the back of every move we make, however mistaken it turns out to be, which we think is in his direction. Our ideas are so often wrong about what he wants of us that perhaps we should go on blindly doing the next thing and not asking to see the pattern and how we are to fit into it. Our mistake is to think of the works we ought to be doing for God, important works which would show us we were serving him in a big way, when all God is thinking of is getting from us the response of love.

But let me get back to the subject of your creative side, your art, because I feel it is bound up with your headlong assault on the religious life. At your conversion and after it you saw an aspect of beauty and truth which, as all artists do, you wanted to catch and reproduce in your own terms. To you it seemed only logical to grasp the good which your newly awakened sense of religion was showing you. And to grasp it at once in case the vision should fade. The nearest fulfilment of beauty and truth in this life was represented to you by the religious life. The monastery crystalised for you, almost guaranteed, the ideal which you had glimpsed. As a painter wants to ensure his inspiration while it lasts—his experience has shown it to be a fleeting thing at best—so you wanted to follow a lead which might not lead for ever. I am not denying that you entered the monastery on the impulse of grace, I am merely saying that what you were really attracted to was an eternal good and that you saw this spelled out exclusively in a temporal one.

You know more about art than I do so I would like your views about that.

Yours,
Dom

Dear X,

So I gather you don't think much of my theory about your art having an effect upon your running off to join a monastery. Directly of course it hasn't, but indirectly I still think it may have. At the risk of boring you with more of what you so sweetly refer to as 'all this mystical nonsense about creative talent and religious vocation' I am going to tell you how the creative urge overreaches itself and lands its unfortunate possessor, unless he is on his guard against it, in every sort of mess: psychologically, morally, spiritually, and even socially. If vocation doesn't come under one or other of those categories where does it come?

The artistic eye—and this applies equally to all creative expressions and not just to the visual arts—sees things at one remove or more from the prototype. Intuitively it apprehends an aspect of reality (or beauty or truth or whatever you like to call that facet of the Absolute which reveals itself to some and not to others) which inevitably is just out of reach. The artist is always one jump ahead of other people in his perceptions and because he can never realise his perceptions in the appropriate medium of his gift he is doomed to fumble, and try and fail, and remain unsatisfied. I'm sure this is why so many artists, poets especially, take to drink. At first their inspiration or vision is pushed along by drink, and they are granted the illusion that they are getting things into true perspective at last and that they are on the way to making actual what they have dimly sensed, but after a bit the opposite takes place and their original vision is clouded. It is at this point that the artist starts drinking not so as to sharpen his vision but to escape from his inability to share his vision. I have known poets and painters who have destroyed themselves and their gifts simply because at one time they thought they could capture what was eluding them and would never admit that absolute beauty must necessarily elude them. So of course shadow had to take the place of substance; reflection had to take the place of that which reflects. And for most artists this is not good enough. Like you they want all or nothing; they refuse to humble themselves and accept the finite (second best) nature God has given them. I suspect that if I had been more of an artist I would have taken to drink long ago. Monks too have a vision beyond their capacity of assimilation, but their training prepares them to face their inadequacy. When artists fail to reproduce their ideal they make the wrong deductions and are made miserable. Monks fail equally to reproduce the ideal but take their failure for granted and try to trust more. But whether you are an artist or a monk, or both, it is the will to keep stretching out to the ideal that matters. Lowering the ideal to the attainable does nobody any good.

Whether you agree with any of this or not the fact remains: you are a man with a spiritual purpose whose circumstances force him to live in a material world. It is a difficult situation to handle and you are sure to make many mistakes. But no amount of mistakes should alter the main issue: your sanctification in the existing setting. Even in the religious life each soul has to mount his own unique climb. So don't be too ready to envy the way of the religious. The religious have not the monopoly. Christ alone is the way and the truth and the life, and he can be followed in the world as faithfully as in the monastery.

Yours, Dom

LETTER 15

Dear X,

By an odd coincidence an hour after I had posted my last letter to you (the one about creative achievement having to lag behind creative vision) I came across a passage in De Vigny in which this line occurs: 'If a man despairs of becoming a poet, let him carry his pack and march in the ranks with the rest of men'. If he despairs of becoming a monk he must do the same. I have been a monk for fifty years, and more or less of an artist for sixty, and have been carrying pack after pack since first I learned to march in the ranks. But I have done so awkwardly, out of step most of the time. I hope this won't be your experience because it is an extremely painful process, the march seeming endless and the packs getting heavier and heavier. Artists (and monks) should not be introverts, and unfortunately this is what most of them are. You question everything, don't you, and you are still doubting God's providence in keeping you in the world when all you want to do is to escape the world and live to him alone. I am always telling people in retreats, and have probably written it in a book or two so you must put up with it if you have heard it from me before, that it is better to be in the wrong box by God's will than in the right box by one's own. In my own life the same mistake has beset me: I have jumped from box to box, always telling myself it was into a safer and holier box, and every time I have discovered, but too late, that I had jumped from selfwill and not with the idea of jumping purely to please God. So I think you will find that if you stay long enough in what you imagine to be the wrong box you will eventually discover that it has been the right one all along.

You remember how you used to laugh at me for going about with a copy of the *Meditations of Marcus Aurelius*? I am still very keen on him but am even keener on Tolstoy—and in fact always have been. Lately I have borrowed a copy of his *Last Diaries* (paperback and easy to get) which I had not read before and am finding immensely interesting. Apart from Harold Nicolson's and James Agate's, most diaries bore my head off—even Pepys's—but Tolstoy's reveals the man's sense of crushing inferiority. Tolstoy inferior! Malcolm Muggeridge put me on to exactly this point about him when we met at the Chester Festival. (M.M. also had some good things to say about Simone Weil whom I know you read and I hope you will re-read, so you will probably get more of her from me in letters to come.) The reason I mention Tolstoy is on account of the same duality in his nature which you yourself experience so keenly. He hates the world but must live in it; he hates himself but is stuck with it; he knows he has the power to produce works which the world recognises to be works of genius, but all the time he sees beyond what the world sees and he is painfully conscious of his inadequacy. One of the most telling glimpses you get of him is when he admits that he has been blessed by God to a remarkable degree, that he has everything a man wants, that he enjoys his family and his riding and his possessions, yet at the same time he is overwhelmed with sadness, is utterly miserable. Isn't this the artist, isn't this the religious man, isn't this the saint or anyway the near-saint? If this sort of thing happens in the life of the greatest creative writer the world has ever known—certainly I would rank him as that—you should not be surprised at feeling unequal to your aspiration.

Yours, Dom

LETTER 16

Dear X,

The eulogy of Tolstoy in my last letter prompted you to make exactly the same criticisms of the great man that were made by his contemporaries—and in fact that were made by himself *of* himself. Nobody was more conscious than he was of the inconsistencies in his life. Probably it was this struggle to reconcile his socialist principles with his landowning aristocratic way of living which killed him. His wife drove him to exasperation and his visitors wasted the time he wanted to give to writing and reading, but it was the ambivalance of his position which finally drove him to leave home and die a few days later. You should read his life. He was tortured by his social conscience but trapped by his tradition. More than anything in the world he wanted peace with God, and the causes to which he was pledged, the people to whom he was tied, the responsibilities which were forced upon him, ruled out, as he saw it, the possibility of peace with God. The more he tried to escape the more his christian conscience, which was as keen as any saint's, dragged him back. Had he lived in the early middle ages, when people didn't bother so much about these things, the clash of principle would not have defeated his spirit, but he lived just at a time when clashes of ideas were coming to a moral collision.

You, I think, would understand this. You are young enough, or old enough, to have seen the inwardness as well as the outwardness of the collision. Don't be too quick to write off Tolstoy as a doctrinaire labour leader living comfortably in an inherited seat as a member of the conservative party.

Do you ever read Kazantzakis? There is an affinity.

Kazantzakis knew more about Homer, and more about the sordid side of life. Nor did he have anything like Tolstoy's genius, but he seems to have shared a parallel struggle. Both were men head and shoulders above writers who were contemporary with them, both were rebels against what would now be called 'the establishment', both were thrown out by the institutions which meant a tremendous lot to them and which they longed to purify. Both were scholars, cultured, deeply religious and with infinite humanity and belief in the perfectibility of man. They shared the same vision, they were crushed by the same frustration and disillusion. Both died as exiles; not as deserters but as misfits and as exiles. Admittedly Kazantzakis lacked Tolstoy's craftsmanship—he probably wrote too fast and much of the material could have been better arranged—but he had the same fire. The Greek was less tender than the Russian, and was more preoccupied with sex. Tolstoy was sensual too, as we know from the biographies which were written about him and from what his wife said about him in letters, but this side of his nature was disciplined, was kept in subjection to the power of even stronger passions, or so I think. Kazantzakis wanted, I rather suspect, to shock. This Tolstoy never wanted to do. Compare Tolstoy's two greatest works of fiction with Kazantzakis's, and you will see how once a master novelist lets himself go beyond the reserves he had set himself he endangers his integrity. Tolstoy never for a moment lost his integrity; with each new book he enhanced it.

This long digression was sparked off by your charging Tolstoy with inconsistency. Of course the accusation is valid. But it applies to his life and not to his work. Aren't we all guilty anyway on both counts? I remember years ago when as a young monk I was advised by Fr Vincent McNabb not to concentrate too much on being consistent or I would make myself miserable and go off my head. It was an odd piece of advice for a senior Dominican to give to a very junior Benedictine, but he explained what he meant. He said that too much self-questioning, too much worrying about the contradictions I saw within myself and all round me would only make it impossible to get on with what I was supposed to be doing. 'You earnest young Benedictines are always bothering about what St Benedict wanted you to be. But whatever you are you are never going to be what St Benedict wanted you to be. Otherwise he would have asked God to put you in the sixth century. Of course you are inconsistent. So am I. The difference between us is that I have come to terms with it and you haven't. I have become consistently inconsistent. You are only inconsistently inconsistent. So what worries you does not worry me in the least. I accept myself as a freak in an order which does not normally produce freaks; you have not accepted yourself as a misfit in an order which is big enough to accommodate misfits'. Now I never admired Fr Vincent in the way which I admired Fr Bede Jarrett, and I never found him half as convincing in his sermons as that other Dominican of his time Fr Hugh Pope, but of the three Fr Vincent had a way of saying things which one didn't forget. The advice helped for many years, when religious orders conformed more or less to their founders' rules, but I can't say that it helps much now. My inconsistency makes me an embarrassment, a misfit, when I am in my monastery and an exile when I am outside it.

But to get back from myself to you. I think you will have to live with your inconsistency. It is the twofold pull of vocation. Only in our Lord and his mother was there no opposing vocational pull, so they could be completely consistent. Where the Father's will is the pattern, the whole and only frame of reference, life becomes very much simpler. Not easier, but simpler. Both the interior and the exterior life come together and in questions of doubt about either there is only one question to ask. On the negative side this cuts out all occasions of sin, and on the positive side develops an unbroken attitude of trust.

Now forget about Tolstoy and Kazantzakis or this correspondence will become a literary discussion and I feel it is meant to be more than an exchange of book lists and a defence of tastes.

Yours as ever,
Dom

Dear X,

I confess your last letter, after the long silence on both our parts, shook me rather. But of course I should have been prepared for the way things have turned out, and even, had I had my wits about me, have expected that before long you would fall in love. So this must mark phase three in your spiritual development. Phase one was your conversion, phase two your supposed vocation to the religious life, and now phase three this apparently overwhelming affair of the heart. (I don't count the times in between as phases because, though they have been formative enough, they didn't demand decisions or the having to face up to a particular summons of grace.) This new development is something which you will have to handle with great care or else all that you have been through so far may be wasted and you could find yourself back in your pre-conversion state. If you were to go back to your worldliness now you would find it far more difficult to extricate yourself this time. The grace would be there but the attraction to respond to it would be less, and having a failure behind you you would have less self-confidence.

From what I have said so far you might think I was against people falling in love, people who are trying to live the interior life I mean, but I can assure you I am not. The complicating factor in your situation is that the girl is already married. That she is older than you are doesn't alter the question either way, but that she is a catholic, has two children, and wants to get a divorce so as to be able to marry you must certainly add to the difficulties. You have not told me whether or not you have committed adultery, but the occasion of doing so is obviously present. Assuming you have not, what is the next move? You know the rules, so presumably you have not written to me in order to hear me repeat them. My job in this can only be to get you to do willingly what the law of God tells you to do on pain of losing your soul's salvation. If you can voluntarily accept the necessity of obeying God and the church you will be using your free will to make the greatest sacrifice a man can make to God. If you voluntarily choose yourself and the girl you will be using your free will to turn against God, the church, religion, your chances of eternal happiness in heaven. You may say it is not as clear cut as that, but in fact it is. You may cite extenuating circumstances of which of course I know nothing—a brutal or an alcoholic or a homosexual husband, the harm done to the children by seeing a marriage which has broken down, the life which could be built up by you into something vastly more pleasing to God than the misery involved as things are— but you can't get round the central fact that marriage is for life and that you are in danger of turning a sacrament into a sacrilege. However you rationalise the course you are wanting to take, and the excuses you see in your favour, a marriage has been witnessed by God and this was not an experiment which would be dependent upon whether it turned out happily or not. 'For better, for worse': her marriage may have turned out for worse but this does not give you or her the power to dissolve it any more than if it had turned out for better you would have the right to judge that married to you she would have made a still better marriage. In this sort of situation it is no good falling back on what is reasonable, what makes for greater happiness, what any amount of other people are doing with their marriage when someone else comes along, or (a very common argument this) that because God is love he knows that human love must override human law. God *is* love, but when human love takes divinely ordered love into its own hands and breaks the laws which govern love there is a split in love. Love can walk out of the love God meant you to share with him and so you walk out of God. If this should happen with you the whole of your spiritual conversion, which was truly a work of grace, might never have happened. Not only would your knowledge of the light be obscured but would work in reverse. Our Lord told the scribes and pharisees that if they had not claimed to have the light they would not have sin, but that boasting of being able to see they had no excuse for refusing what their vision showed them.

If I sound harsh and censorious in this letter, please remember I am deeply sympathetic and, so far as I can be without knowing all the circumstances, truly confident and understanding.

As ever—and I mean this—

Dom

Dear X,

It is good of you to tell me more about how this relationship started and how it has developed. Also it is a relief to know that 'nothing has happened'—as they say—between you. But the position is obviously fraught with danger and every meeting between you and the girl is going to be extremely tricky. A book has recently (1974) come out by Karl Menninger, who is a doctor, and I suppose a psychiatrist, called *Whatever Became of Sin*. It is very much in the modern idiom and a lot of it I don't agree with at all, but there's a paragraph on the subject of adultery which lights up a point I had not thought of before. 'Adultery is less "sinful" for its sexual content than for its violation of trust and integrity. Indeed the sin of infidelity, of personal disloyalty to a spouse, to a family, to a friend, to *trusting* friends, to students— this we should surely record as a major sin ... I would emphasise the kind of infidelity and broken trust which may not break the law but does break the heart'. Of course he leaves out the essential quality of the sin so far as the catholic is concerned—namely that it is an offence against God—but at least he recognises the social and personal harm it does over and above the harm it does to the two adulterers themselves. This is often forgotten by people who come to one in the confessional, and it is this, as well as the sexual transgression and the specifically sinful aspect of it as it is seen by God, which you will have to think about when the relationship is getting near to the edge. (I have looked up Menninger, and it seems he *is* a psychiatrist and apparently a well known one. To judge from the authorities he quotes I doubt if he is a catholic. The passage, in case you have to look it up and go on from there—though adultery or even sex forms only a small part of the book—is on page 140.)

But to take up the points you are asking about in your letter, some of which are rather too intimate to be gone into by letter and could wait until we have a chance of meeting and talking about them, there is first of all the guilt or lack of guilt involved in a man being in love with a married woman. In itself I would say the guilt depends not upon what has happened to you psychologically, which unless you have gone out of your way to start it up is beyond your control, but what you have done to encourage it and put opportunities of gratifying the pleasure of it in your way. It is easy enough to generalise about this sort of attachment but so much depends on the people concerned, on the safeguards they are applying, on whether they share the same conscience on the thing, on whether both are praying and trying to advance in prayer, and so on, that apart from laying down the code of behaviour to be observed, which you know already, I doubt if I can help. Of course you may not want to write about it again, and I would not blame you if you didn't, but if you are looking for suggestions, and particularly for how spiritual principles apply, then it might be as well to let me know to what extent religion plays any real part in this other person's life, to what extent she would accept your ruling on how to go about the affair, on whether she would be prepared to call the whole thing off if it developed into a serious occasion of sin for either of you. If even this sounds too academic, why not ask her to tell you honestly how it is affecting her relationship with her husband, her children, her prayer. If she is not a person of prayer it makes the whole thing much more difficult for both of you.   Yours, Dom

Dear X,

Oh I see. It hasn't come to anything. But may I add the possibly hurtful word 'yet'? There is nothing on earth that can so fool people into believing that over this love business they are safe. Nobody is safe. Every morning and a dozen times a day you have to remind yourself that love comes from God and must go back to God, and that in the meantime there must be no playing about with a love that leaves God out. The only real infidelity, I think, whether about love or about anything else in life, is to leave God out. And when love drops below a certain level the big temptation is to leave God out. The next big temptation is to pretend you haven't. God *is* love and cannot be left out of himself. When he is left out of himself it is not love at all but lust, and when indulged or even condoned, lust has no part with the spiritual life which you are trying to lead. Love is such a subtle emotion that the lightest touch can send it off balance, and the effect of deflecting it from the true has the fatal effect of diverting its direction towards the false.

To claim that human love is an aspect of divine love is not a piece of trickery, is not a fabrication on the part of moral and spiritual theologians to make human love sound respectable. Unless it is seen as such, unless in actual experience it is felt to bring the soul nearer to God and to God's love as expressed in charity towards others, it is not a love which can be safely dabbled with by people who are trying to live the interior life. Indeed I doubt if it can be safely dabbled with at all unless God comes in to make a third in the relationship. But it would be difficult to persuade people of this. The lower emotions of love, clamouring for excitement and sex at the wrong level and to the exclusion of the appetite's satisfaction at the right level, can so obscure the issue as to leave the mind confused and the physical desires even more roused than they were before. This is why prayer is so important here, not to provide a cover which gives the soul a sense of justification as if providing a free pass which exonerates from any little guilty actions which take place along the way, but because it is only by the light of prayer that the soul comes to see how love is essentially a unity, and only accidentally a separator which leads to sin on the one side and sanctity on the other. Prayer shows too how charity to others is God acting out his charity to us, how ideally there are not two charities but one. And that God is the one.

I think perhaps the greatest sin is to deprive God of something which he not only contains and owns but which he actually is. For instance God owns the beauty of creation, contains the justice of law, orders history by his providential wisdom, infallibly guides his church. But much worse than desecrating nature, breaking laws, questioning his action in the unfolding of history or in the pope's inerrancy where faith and morals are concerned is to steal God's love and put it to an unworthy use. Once we understand that God assumes responsibility for being love, the lesser love is incorporated in the greater: they are identified. So for a human being to exercise a proprietory right over a human love is to deny not only an attribute of God but God himself. Fortunately people don't realise this when they are loving selfishly, or even not loving at all and just satisfying their physical appetites, but this is what it amounts to and, if we had our wits about us at the time, what we would have to accuse ourselves of. But you may not agree with half this.   Yours, Dom

Dear X,

Before waiting for an answer to my last letter (the one about the twofold activity of what is ideally one : the single force expressing itself in two, and often in opposite, ways), I would like to illustrate the theme with something which came into my mind after what I had written. It may serve to show what I was driving at and even if it doesn't say what I want to say it can hardly confuse a theme which to anyone who has read as much as you have read must seem patently obvious. You know how ignorant I am of anything which has to do with mechanics but I seem to remember a system of refuelling in the air, which may still be in use for all I know, whereby a tanker plane fed oil (or petrol) to a smaller plane while still in the air by means of some sort of flexible pipe or tube. The point to be made here is that while human love is possessed of enough fuel to raise itself above the earth, above the gritty dirty surface of earthly desire, it cannot stay in the skies for ever. Either it has to come down (like Pegasus) and store up more power, or it has to remain grounded for good and make no further attempt at flight, or it has to get its fuel from above. In the suggested image God is the source of supply. God is the supply, and if love is to exist at all it has to be fed through him with the staying power which comes from him and must *be* him. Of course like all illustrations the image fails to cover the fact that there are not two vessels to be filled, two tanks, but one. All I am trying to say is that in the love affair of yours which you are wanting to keep on the highest plane you cannot afford to let the supply come from the lower source but must be constantly in communication with the higher. And this can only be done in the life of prayer and in fidelity to the church's sacramental life. Otherwise you will make a mess of it. Human love inheres in divine love, and to force a division is to define a new thing: a human thing if you like but not the kind of human thing which goes with the spiritual life which you are trying to lead.

There has been too much talk in recent years about human love taking precedence over every duty, every call, every vocational grace. But the only claim which human love can make is in the name of divine love from which it derives its being. Once you give human love its paramount demand, there is nothing in the world which will keep it within bounds. Put it in its proper element and there is nothing in the world which will tell you more about God.

Don't think I am being censorious about this attachment of yours. Many would say I am being strict. But leave out strictness and the only controls are your own inclinations. As well as inclination there is of course conscience, and conscience can act as a brake, but how often is not conscience led along the way marked out by inclination? If conscience is to be valid—and in matters of the heart it is extremely difficult for conscience to act validly—it has to be informed by law and by the light of grace. All too often it is informed by desire and the law of majority opinion. I know you cannot forget about your desires at a time when you are powerfully in love with someone but you should be able to detach yourself from the majority opinion. The majority opinion is of the earth, earthy, and you are of the spirit.

Yours,
Dom

Dear X,

I have now had your answer to my last two letters. Many thanks. Forgive me if I go on and on about this attachment of yours because I feel from what you are now telling me about it you are rationalising it to yourself. Once we start developing the art of special pleading—which we do at every opportunity, as I would be the first to admit in the matter of spending a great deal of time outside my monastery—the pleading becomes cajoling. You can argue on good evidence —temporary evidence as it must be since the thing has not been going on for long—that this sinless attachment has helped you spiritually and morally, and that as far as you can see it has had the came effect on her. This is something which cannot be judged by such tests as you might apply to almost any activity outside that of love itself. Though, as I have tried to show, divine and human love are one in origin and being, this does not prevent human love from breaking away while pretending to inhere in its substance. Human love, because it comes from Love itself, cannot afford to break away. When human love breaks away it destroys itself. Remember how Harpagon discovered the use of gold as one of the goods of life, and how from this it became to him the object of consuming desire, and how the deprivation of it spelled death. We can start by valuing love for what it is, but later it can become an obsession which claims first place over everything, and later still it can destroy us because we find we cannot do without it. It may spell death but we would rather have death than sacrifice it and live. I am putting that side of it to you only that you should take all the greater care to ensure the other side. There is nothing like human love when it comes to deceiving us about our true motives. 'When a human being is necessary to us' wrote Simone Weil in one of her essays, 'We cannot desire that person's good unless we cease to desire our own.' Only the honest can find it in themselves to answer that test in their favour. The words to look at in the quotation are 'necessary' and 'good'. I grant you that the love of this girl may have become necessary to you but I wonder whether this necessity has lasted long enough for you to judge about the desire which you have for her good and how far you can cease to calculate your own. If human relationships are to run satisfactorily, let alone sinlessly, there has to be an identity of purpose. Admittedly the degree of affection will not be the same in each person, and ideals unfortunately will differ, but when one or other is attracted by the idea of personal advantage there can be no real harmony and very little chance of permanence.

You wrote in your letter that seeing one another often had become for you both a 'necessity'. It is just this that scares me. If true, it will mean a number of things which do not fit comfortably into her vocation as wife and mother any more than it will fit comfortably into your vocation to serve God in the spiritual life. I know your place is in the world and not in the monastery; I know that for her there may be greater freedom in expressing human affection than there would be, for instance, in the case of a nun. But even so . . . People are always saying to people they love 'I only want you to be happy; I really don't care about myself' but I wonder how many of them really mean it. Don't you think what they really mean is: 'I do want you to be happy, but I also want you to know that it is I who am making you happy. I don't want you to forget that in trying to forget myself I am trying to add to your happiness'.   Yours, Dom

Dear X,

You talk about this 'friendship' which exists between a married woman and yourself. But are you not slightly, if unconsciously, fooling yourself? Forgive me for being pedantic but Pythagoras defines friendship as 'an equality made of harmony'. The harmony here is between two dissimilar natures, even perhaps between opposite natures. But in your particular situation we are talking not of natures but of vocations; we are talking of two quite different ways of life, one married and one single. She is committed to her family, you are committed to the interior life. Such harmony as exists between the two of you—I mean in your relationship rather than in your attitudes towards morality, religion, duty and so on—is the outcome (and a perfectly healthy one I can assure you) of a shared desire to preserve two things: personal autonomy and the freedom to handle the situation which has arisen between you. Now though the desire is to share, however unselfish the desire there is inevitably an imbalance, since not only are no two people the same but no two loves are the same. This imbalance has to be allowed for, and very often the reason why relationships break up and marriages come to grief is because the imbalance has not been allowed for and the personal autonomy on the part of one member has dominated and so restricted the freedom which should be maintained on the part of the other. I know it could be objected that the appropriate expression of love is sacrifice and that therefore the more you renounce your autonomy and your freedom the better, but there is nevertheless a small secret area of the soul into which God's claim alone can come and where alone God's claim can be met. People in the world, just as people in religion, can give themselves to God. The vocation to do so is to all. But if we are talking about chastity being preserved between two people (which is what we *are* talking about: she married and you single) we are talking about something sacred. Chastity is something more than being single if you happen not to have a wife or if you are a widower: it is that something, that reservation, which makes you wholly God's. Even chastity between husband and wife, belonging as they do to one another, is something freely given to God within the vocation to matrimony.

Of course there are good catholics, whether married or single, who would not agree with what I have just been saying. But remember you have asked me to help you in scaling the heights. Love between two people one of whom is married is such a tricky business that unless both have a pretty clear view of the heights there is likely to be a lot of thin ice in the valleys. I think you have to distinguish between reciprocity of affection, which is obviously present here, and mutual appreciation of an ideal. I mean it does not necessarily follow that because you respect one another's moral principles, and even reverence one another's bodies to the extent of disclaiming rights to which, in this particular relationship, you have no right, you are as one in your concept of christian chastity. But then of course I have not met the other person. For all I know she may be leading you up to the heights which are far above what you have been hoping to attain to with help from me. If so, let her lead on. As a climbing instructor I gladly retire.

Yours as ever,

Dom

Dear X,

Your letter telling me that no amount of theorising could alter the fact that the love of God and the love of a person were two different things did not surprise me. In your present state and in the present relationship you could hardly be expected to recognise the unity of love. Because we are fallen creatures all human love is bound to have an element of earthiness about it, but having admitted this and faced the implication of being tempted through the senses there still remains the truth that since love comes from God and must go back to him the human element can be raised until it meets the divine. What you are suffering from is an awareness of the body to the exclusion, or at least to the temporary forgetting, of the spirit. Don't forget we are not made, as the angels are, in one piece. We are made, as our first parents were, body and soul. When the body rebelled against the superiority of the soul a division took place which not even Christ's atonement brought back to fusion. Integrity was lost with original sin and since that moment the soul has been hard put to it to keep the body from claiming dominion. Naturally, in nature's fallen state, your desire to possess the whole of this girl whom you are in love with, includes the appetite for physical satisfaction. It could not be otherwise. But as well as the bodily attraction—and it is always the physical appeal which is first perceived since it is the senses which are responsible for registering to the mind and emotions—there are other activities at work, and these, because they operate at a deeper level, are often denied the credit for being there at all. If the mutual attraction were all flesh and nothing else you would have fallen into sin long ago. But because you have not done this it is clear that in addition to the physical magnetism which is inevitable there are the other qualities which both charm and exercise a controlling influence. I find it difficult not to sound pompous in saying this but the qualities to be developed, apart from the obvious one of self-denial in anything which has to do with physical contact, are compassion, honest criticism, detachment in the use of time, making allowances for the female psyche, suppression of the least jealousy, and infinite patience and trust. This is a formidable list but you will see how vital to the safety of the relationship each of its points must be.

Anyway you cannot charge me this time with not being practical enough in the advice I give. Short of telling you how many minutes you should allow yourself in your telephone conversations and how many inches should separate you when you and she dine together I could hardly be more specific. But I still think that if you look more deeply and prayerfully into the principles of love—love as the virtue of charity—you will find the application working out according to the theory. It is only when we force the theory to fit in with a particular line of conduct or, which is just as bad, when we take the laws of conduct into our own hands and forget about the theory, that we find ourselves in trouble. But there will probably be more about this in my next letter.

Yours,
Dom

LETTER 24

Dear X,

There was one passage in your letter (I might as well be frank) which infuriated me. It showed me you had completely missed the point of what I have been writing to you for weeks. It was where you said 'After all her husband is running round with someone else so I need not feel too bad about my much milder deviation from the book'. This is just the kind of cynical, worldly, capitulating, generally accepted attitude which I hoped your prayer life would dismiss instantly. If you cannot rise above that sort of excuse you cannot expect to see what human-divine love really means. The safeguards cannot be counted upon to stand up against that sort of argument. If all the husbands in the world were unfaithful it would not give you the right to have an affair with the wife of a single one of them. What you are admitting is that your understanding of human love is unrelated to all that you have been learning for years about divine love. Do bear in mind that God came into your life in a very special way at a particular time—at a time when you were not paying him much attention if you remember—and that this carries with it a responsibility of judging love on his terms and not in terms of the divorce court, the popular play, the glossy magazine.

Without having to bother about telling you that you are loving badly, stupidly, incompletely, I can stick simply to the fact that you have missed the meaning of the basic text 'God is love'. Until you recognise the implications of this statement you will go on making lunatic comments such as you made in your letter about the girl's husband giving himself greater liberty than you are giving to yourself. Has he had your

graces? Does it serve him right if his wife prefers someone else? Is love to be graded according to the offences
that it allows against itself?

Here is an illustration (not a very good one but
it will show you what I mean). A family is starving in
the desert and the mother dies. The baby is crying
out for its mother's milk. The father can explain that
there is no milk to be had but the baby goes on crying
for milk. The father may give the baby a tin of petrol
to drink or a flask of brandy, but this won't help because if there is no milk the baby will die. All of us
are thirsty for love. We are not going to be saved by
petrol or brandy because what we need is milk. People
can tell us until they are black in the face that all we
want is liquid of some sort, liquid of any sort, and we
won't be thirsty any more. Up to a point they are
right: momentarily the thirst is met. But unless the
thirst is met with the liquid which it is meant to have
it will be worse off than it was before, worse off than
if there were nothing at all. To make the story even
more depressing I might add that for the father to tell
the baby that its thirst was purely imaginary, that it
mustn't make such a fuss, that what it really needed
was a good sleep would only complicate the matter.
The baby, quite rightly, would go on crying. Now sit
down for five minutes and think of what the world
does to meet the need for love. No wonder we all cry
too much.

As always—in spite of my angry tone,

Dom

Dear X,

I cannot blame you for drawing the inferences which you did from my last letter. Thinking back at what I wrote I can see how your criticism is justified and how you find me unfeeling on the subject about which you feel more deeply than any other. At once let me correct an impression. The misunderstanding has arisen on account of what both of us have referred to for years as your 'conversion'. In your present involvement—which though not technically guilty because nothing has 'happened' is decidedly romantic and therefore between a single and a married person not altogether according to the book—you may not attach to your conversion the importance which you once did. I attach enormous importance to it (and don't forget I am a pro). This being so I think: (a) you are taking great risks, and (b) you are failing to grasp the essential connection between God and his creatures, between divine and human love, between marital and extra-marital relationship. Got that?

Now. God's finger has touched you. This is nothing revivalist, has nothing of Elmer Gantry about it. Among those to whom this happens a new code is born. I'm sorry but you can't get out of it by saying it was just an emotional experience, the kind of thing that happens in a retreat. For you it was no illusion. It was real. True contact with God is not just a luxury: it has to be followed up. My own personal opinion is that it was granted to you so that you might be prepared for this very close relationship, and that you would be in a position to see where your first duty must lie. I am not altogether happy about how you have applied the logic of this. Different people argue in different ways on this subject. Some, realising that God has laid his finger on them, jump to the conclusion that material things, natural affection, created beauty and so on have no further significance for them any more. Others feel that from now onwards the whole of their lives must be spent in a succession of observances, if only to ensure the fidelity to which their spiritual experience has pledged them. Surely the lesson to be drawn is this: the point of material things, human relationship, natural goodness and wellbeing is to raise the mind from the physical to the spiritual. 'The things that are seen are temporal; the things that are not seen are eternal'. St Paul further reminds us that not to go on from the temporal to the eternal in our process of thought is inexcusable. Many religious people are so obsessed with pushing the argument to the eternal that they have nothing but scorn for the temporal. It is no compliment to God to lump created things together—nature, friends, art, the liturgy, scholarship and science—and treat them as unimportant. Relative realities should not be disdained simply because they do not happen to match the absolute. In the light of the absolute they should be thought of as more real, not less. This lecture I'm boring you with is meant to show you that relative, temporal, human, emotional and physical love cannot be risked. Nothing can be risked on the grounds that the absolute from which it derives is the only thing you have to bother about. The more you bother about the absolute the more careful you have to be in preserving the integrity of the relative. I have something else to say about this affair of yours but I'm keeping it until I write again. This is partly because you have had about enough of my attacking you for being obtuse, and partly because I want to give myself more time to think and pray about what I am going to say.

Yours still with infinite sympathy,
Dom

Dear X,

In the ordinary way I am against abruptly breaking off associations such as yours which are harmless if handled properly but potentially harmful. The drawback to making the grand renunciation is that it tends to be made between inverted commas, and that where the dramatic assumes more importance than the real there is no guarantee that the real will remain strong enough to sustain the weight of time. Also there is not only the danger of serious reaction—not being able to stick to the plan of separation and as a result overdoing the reunion, which might be disastrous—but of the increased tension in the imagination. When people who have been seeing a lot of each other, are over-fond of each other, decide to part and not see one another again or write or telephone, there is a void which has to be filled somehow. Work helps, change of scene which avoids associations and memories helps, meeting people who are not likely to open up on the subject of the broken romance helps. But these are felt to be the most superficial of substitutes, and the moment the mind is free it goes over all that has happened and adds a lot more that may have happened: suspicions, regrets, jealousies, speculations about how the other person is taking it. All this can become more harmful to one's peace of mind, and more unhealthy if the theme runs at all to sensuality as of course it must, than if one were seeing the person every day and carrying on the relationship along lines that had become almost normal.

These anyway would be my reasons for not making a sudden and final break. The spectacular is always suspect, and there is nothing so spectacular to the romantic imagination as the heroic gesture, particularly if 'it is for your sake, my dear, and for your marriage . . . please don't think of me, I don't matter a bit.' But this said, there may be situations which do in fact call for the complete break. I can think of a few straight off: the recurrence of temptations which amount to occasions of sin, the demand on the husband's part, the disturbance caused to one's God-given vocation and work, the liability of furtive deception, the threat to mental balance, the neglect of overriding responsibility. So in your situation (I hate using the words 'case' and 'predicament' because 'case' always suggests the textbook and 'predicament' always suggests an embarrassment of some sort, whereas this affair of yours carries a significance which is beyond generalisation and regulation) I think the time has come for you to weigh up as objectively as possible—which is a silly thing to say because the whole point of the thing is subjective and the issue to be decided is conditioned by two people's reactions to it—and to decide how each of you would benefit spiritually and psychologically in choosing either course. Take a good look at the parable of the wheat and the cockle before you make a decision about this. And try to see her field as well as yours. You may, with the best intention in the world, be uprooting more than you know. Fields which are left half empty are likely to grow stronger crops of cockle than before. Pray that you and she may agree as to the best thing to be done before God. This is what really matters. If you do his will one way or the other in the course you take, you may sure that he will look after the effect it has upon the husband, the children, your vocation and hers. At least so I think.

Joining you in asking for light on this,

Dom

Dear X,

So you have decided not to see one another again. Or write or telephone. It is a brave decision to make and I hope you will keep to it. Don't make exceptions for birthdays, Christmas, personal anniversaries. As in giving up alcohol for good there can be no special occasions. This business of a complete break has never worked with me—I have either gone back on it or it has ended in a breakdown—but I think you are a stronger character than I am and in any case will recover more quickly. If partings have to happen it is better they should happen before the hurt is too great to be borne. I always think Theseus showed good sense in getting clear of Medea at once, and Aegeus, who was not really in on the story, was right to say 'It is hard enough to face sorrow when it comes. Let us not discuss it now'. So I will not discuss the sorrow you must be feeling unless you bring it up yourself.

I hope you are back at work, writing and painting. One has to flog oneself at first after an interval but it is worth it. The results themselves may be bad, but they get better. Don't let anyone talk to you about a 'writer's block' or a painter's need to lie fallow for a bit and look at the masterpieces. Inspiration is not nearly as necessary as self-discipline where the creative arts are concerned. The great thing is to avoid the sense of defeat. People like you and me don't make enough of the corrupting influence of erosion. After an unhappy love affair the temptation to sit back and think is as serious as to let cynicism take over. I would rather be angry, assertive, self-opinionated and wrong than be supine and right. That is why I am not in the least disturbed by your present antagonism to the changes in the church. This seems to me far healthier than assuming the passive attitude which so many catholics assume : namely that whatever has come out of Vatican II is what the Holy Spirit meant to come out of it. Obviously the Holy Spirit was at work in drawing up the decrees, but there is no guarantee that the decrees have been rightly interpreted. Nobody is going to persuade me that the council or the Holy Father meant parish priests to release a hundred balloons at the *Gloria* on Christmas Day instead of ringing the bells and singing the thing in Latin—which is still, as Pope Paul repeatedly insists, the official language of the church. At a parish where I had recently to attend mass during the Christmas season, the priest began the sacrifice of Calvary with 'Well, folks, have a nice day' and ended with 'Be seeing you during the week I hope, friends, and go easy on the booze'. The vulgarity of the post-Vatican church drives me frantic, but once we accept the truth of the church we have to learn to take the vulgarities, the anomalies, the fatuities in our stride. (The crib was arranged at the cathedral—the cathedral mind you, the seat of episcopal authority—so that the *mensa* of the mass was at the same time the flat roof of the cave or stable.) Fortunately I am allowed to say the Latin mass each day, and I notice that since the local people have got to know about this an increasing number of people come to it. If you could see the way the religious life is developing in this country you would not regret having left the novitiate while the going was good. Curiously the monks are better than the sisters. Some sisters came to a retreat of mine last week some of whom wore expensive wigs, skirts which bordered on immodesty and pink nail varnish. They can hardly have liked my retreat.

Yours always,

Dom

Dear X,

Since it is clear that you feel as I do about the changes in the church and in the religious communities of the more progressive stripe you will be interested to know that about a third of my mail every day is made up of letters from people who complain bitterly of some of the innovations and who beg me to do something in the way of whipping up an opposition. But what can I do beyond urging these correspondents (most of whom I have never met) to hang on and pray for a return to older ways? Many have written to say that they do not go to mass any more and that even their children are looking for deeper interpretations of the new rites than they are getting from the pulpit. This seems to me highly significant since we were told a few years ago that the liturgical changes were introduced largely in order to attract the young. The demand now, from both young and old, is that there should be more time during the mass for private prayer and that apart from the short sitting-down interlude after holy communion there is always a noise of some sort going on. (I like Bruce Marshall's phrase about the 'theft of silence from a world already dedicated to din'.) Not long ago I was sent a cutting from a paper which told of school-children being herded into a cafeteria where mass was celebrated on the counter: 'The children would more easily appreciate the last supper in a more appropriate setting than the chapel'. I felt like writing back to say that the children would appreciate the last supper even better if they attended reclining or lying down. Guitars were allowed but not missals and the priest wore no vestments. The chalice was a china cup and instead of altar breads there were brown wholemeal loaves which were crumbled up and distributed. I am glad I was not there.

In the conventual life you find much the same thing going on. I have in front of me as I write an illustration from a magazine which shows a Benedictine sister 'styling' a model's hair. The sister, the caption informs us, 'is studying hair-styling for service as a consultant to the members of her order. The Benedictine Sisters . . . adopted a new religious habit which makes its members' hair visible. Sister Josephine, who was a hair-dresser before entering the order, took a refresher course at Ricky's School of Beauty Culture in Joliet and is now actively engaged as a hair style consultant for the order'. Are you turning in your grave, St Benedict? Or having your beard trimmed and curled?

In February 1972 the Vatican explicitly forbade nuns to 'discard religious garb' for lay dress. This has simply not been obeyed. Instead of complying, certain congregations of sisters have compromised by wearing a cross or a religious emblem of some sort such as many wear today who have no religious commitment whatever. Now even religious emblems are considered—with no backing from authority—to be unnecessary. No wonder vocations are scarce. Possible applicants are hesitating between those religious orders which their progressive friends tell them are dead and others which have no authority to be born. You may live to see a return to orthodox religious life —though not I imagine to the divine office as it used to be (in Latin and with prime as one of the hours)— but I certainly shall not. There is no harm in praying for such a return, and working for it. This is all I can do now.

Revirescit . . . I hope.

Dom

Dear X,

Reading your letter—with its criticisms as frank as mine about the abuses in the post-Vatican council church—I was particularly interested to see the different way in which you and I approach the question. I feel yours is the more profound view, and that when things come right again it will be because lay people and ecclesiastics alike have gone about it in your way rather than in mine. Where you see the church as a structure, a divinely appointed organisation with a hierarchy and a policy and a social conscience guided by the Holy Spirit, I see it more as an organism made up of cells which have their own personal responsibility of accepting or rejecting authority and tradition. I think yours is the safer understanding of the church's place in the world because it bases the whole conception on truth; mine, more individualistic, tends to pick on the anomalies and consequently fails in charity and patience. Where you are concerned, and rightly, about the overall drift from submission, about the questioning of doctrines and institutions which have been accepted for centuries, I worry more about what is being taught in the seminaries, about the defections among priests and religious, about the drop in vocations, about questions of monastic observance and the ideas prevalent regarding formation and prayer and the value of liturgical worship. I find that words which ought to mean a great deal, and which should be followed up by the whole church acting together—such as 'renewal', 'reconciliation', 'ecumenism' and so on—have come to mean very little indeed. And this can only mean that the Vatican council, for all the lead that it gave, has been singularly disappointing in its effects.

Such a lot of life consists in waiting for things to happen, waiting for them to take a turn for the better, and they very seldom do. I am beginning to think that the whole of this life is meant to be a lesson in patience. Patience, compassion, fortitude: they come to the same thing in the end. We hope for certain results which we think are due, results to which we have a right, but the results are either deferred indefinitely or other things are substituted for them. Often the results are not what we hoped for at all, are what we dreaded. But this must not be allowed to crush us: it is the incentive and very stuff of trust. It is all a matter of waiting, trusting, listening to the voice of the Spirit. In this sense the ultimate fulfilment of our hope is inevitable. To replace hope and trust with anything less is a betrayal, a desertion. Remember the story of Electra and Orestes. Electra was sure that the object of all her hope was finished, that Orestes no longer existed. But she did not go back to her old life. She chose the memory of Orestes with all its loneliness rather than the presence of those who would have tried to compensate. Orestes had promised much but delivered nothing. The nothing of Orestes was preferable to the everything of others. When Orestes was sure of this he came back. Her blind and lonely trust was justified. The whole story is very like Mary Magdalen and the risen Christ. 'Rabboni' she said. One day the faithful, which means the trusting, will see an end to their waiting and will be able to say to the church 'Rabboni'. Orestes is here all the time.

Confidently,
Dom

Dear X,

Your letter, I admit, saddened me rather. You say you have not been going to mass any more on account of the changes, and that it is better to stay away than to spend the half hour in a state of exasperation and resentment. What surprises me is that a priest has sanctioned this on condition you read the mass as printed in the old missal at some other time or at home. This seems to me a very odd permission to give, but that's his business and not mine. Perhaps you have told him, as you have now told me, that you will not regard yourself responsible for leaving the church altogether if things go on the way they do. This, though I am sure you meant what you said, probably blackmailed him into giving the permission he did. It would not have blackmailed me.

But let me touch on the other point for a minute, namely your not being held responsible for leaving the church. Isn't this what we all say when we are hell-bent on following our own will? We build up an excuse, rationalise and emotionalise it, and then talk about not being accounted responsible. This is surely a combination of subjectivism and the situation ethic. It means that obedience can be brushed aside if one's inner compulsions are strong enough. Obedience is to something outward, compulsions come from something inward. The inward has always to be checked against the outward or law and authority become meaningless. Each soul has a responsibility to act in a particular way irrespective of social pressure, prejudice, temptation, obsession, worldly opinion, personal bent (what a good word 'bent' is in this context). 'Compulsions' can be blown up in the imagination to a point when there is no longer a moral imperative. You have your compulsions, I have mine. But if they were to be taken literally—as positively compelling— where would be conscience, freewill, grace, the ten commandments? I wonder how far either of us is influenced in matters of serious responsibility by what is called a compulsion. I hope not much. You tell me in your letter that it won't be your fault if you leave a church which has let you down. In the same way I try to tell myself it won't be my fault if I end a life which has let me down, never brought me happiness, never even been chosen by me—in the sense that had I been given the option before birth I would certainly not have chosen to be born—yet I know well I am not under a compulsion to commit suicide. Just as for you the desire to leave the church as a disappointed and would-be good catholic, so for me the desire to take my life as a disappointed and resentful human being has to be referred to the objective situation decreed by the providence of God. The church exists and is true and must be obeyed; my life exists and must be lived. A catholic may love the church or hate it; a man may love life or hate it. The church and life are facts, whatever we feel about them. The only way to live the catholic life is to live it in Christ. Given the necessity of a human life, the only way for the possessor to live it is to live it in Christ. We are back again at what I was saying in a recent letter about waiting. So long as we remain calm, and grace enables us to remain calm, we can each of us persevere in the state arranged for us by a God who knows better than we do what is good for us—what is good for us in the long term, I mean, and so what is good for our eternal salvation—but there is no guarantee that to remain calm, even with the help of grace, is going to be easy.

You may reach desperation point with regard to the church, I may reach desperation point with regard to continued existence. Grace is never in desperation. More about this in another letter . . . as ever,

Dom

Dear X,

Your reply to my last letter was different from what I was expecting. You seemed to understand what I was saying. But in expressing sympathy for my habitual antagonism to life—to my own life, that is, and not to life in general which I know to be a good—you have made me feel guilty of self-pity. So I must quickly correct this. I'm sure I am to blame. I do not pity myself in the least, and I certainly do not blame anybody else. It is just the way I happen to be made and I am confident that God makes allowances for the freaks of his creation. So it is not self-pity which is at the back of this so much as self-knowledge. I can seriously and sincerely say that since about the age of six I have never enjoyed life—and would never wish for one single day of it back—but against this I have no resentment towards God for the way he has mapped this out. That's his affair. All I am saying is that for sixty-four years I have not liked it a bit and would wish it had never been. I mentioned my *malaise* in my last letter to you only because I hoped you would compare your half-hour's attendance at the English modern mass with sixty four-years' attendance at a disagreeable life and this would enable you to draw a parallel conclusion. We are expected to do what we have to do, and neither enjoyment nor devotion truly signify. It is only the will that matters, the will to go ahead accepting God's will. Once we bow to God's will—whether it is in the church or in life or in circumstances or in suffering or in people or in history, science, politics, or the future—we have got it made, as the Americans say. And this is what I pray daily you may experience. It is harder for you than for me.

You are younger for one thing, and young people naturally want the will of God to be presented in literary form, defined and explained, applicable to every contingency. This kind of ruling about many moral and liturgical issues—even to the interpretation of the miraculous element in the scriptures and to the kind of belief demanded by dogma—has almost entirely gone. It is rapidly becoming a free for all 'and let conscience be your guide'. Older people look back wistfully at what they enjoyed all too uncaringly but I think they probably take for granted that they will never experience again the satisfaction they felt in religion. Also they feel they have less time ahead of them in which to endure their dissatisfaction. Young and old are equally puzzled by what is going on in the church but where the young are angry the old are disappointed.

Where we have to be careful is in avoiding what Irving Janis calls the 'group-think'. Group-think makes honest exchange of thought impossible, and what we need more than anything in the church just now is a willingness to understand the workings of the minds of the opposition. I do not mean here the collective mind of the opposition—because this would only mean two group-thinks instead of one, and we know anyway what the opposition thinks—but that we should be ready to rise above the stereotyped view. Once we assume that consensus of opinion is inevitably the opinion to be followed we are abrogating our freewill, our conscience, our right to protest. Unity is a good but unanimity, which is group-thinking in triumph, is a god. Group-thinking means slavery in the end.

More to come but not now,

as ever   Dom

Dear X,

Your letter shows clearly how deeply miserable you are. I feel for you with all my heart, and whatever I say in this letter or in any other is said in sympathy and not in accusation. I do not accuse you either of handling things in the wrong way since your conversion or of giving in to self pity. What I think we must both of us concentrate on when in deep sorrow is control of the emotions. This sounds fairly obvious but what I mean is that it is not the misery which is the main thing but the endurance. Misery is a passion, endurance is a strength. At the time it does not help to know this, but misery of itself is no virtue—though it can be made into one by being identified with our Lord's passion—whereas endurance for Christ's sake is a part of faith, hope, love, acceptance and perseverance. You and I have been given a great opportunity here and we must not spoil the quality of our respective endurances with resentment. The temptation for you is to hold it against God that the grace of your conversion has landed you in nothing but suffering; the temptation for me is to hold it against him that he caused me to be born in the first place when I could have been spared so much if I had been simply left out of existence. We both in our different ways endure —partly because we have to—so the value of our endurance depends on our willingness.

You hinted in your last letter that your endurance might quite well snap. I don't for a moment think it will. The determination to endure is so much part of it that nothing short of desperation amounting to loss of reason and freewill could abrogate it. Of course you could choose to go back on all that the grace of your conversion has taught you, just as I could let my loathing for life exhaust my rational judgment, destroy my will to persevere, but there is always the fact of grace which has to be taken into account. Grace does not normally permit a *dementia* to alter the direction of a deliberately chosen course and reverse the whole process of sanctification. If the *dementia* were genuine—were strictly madness—then obviously the consequences of such decisions would not be culpable. Neither of us is mad. We are only angry at what has fallen to our lot. The church is *there,* existence is *there.* Respectively we are stuck with these things; they are facts. The sooner we adapt ourselves to them the better. You may imagine you would be better off not being converted, I may imagine I would be better off not being alive, but the point is that each of us has to reckon with the providence of God. The church is true, life has to be led. So we get on with what we have been given. I don't think it matters much your having a different view from me about either the church or life. I do think it matters that we agree on swallowing God's will whole and making the best of it.

The other day I was sitting alone in a parked car saying my prayers and waiting for the owner to come back from some errand and drive on. The only human being in sight was a small boy aged about three licking an icecream cone. He hadn't seen me so didn't know I was watching him. It was up in the mountains. Snow everywhere, sunshine, bright blue sky. The little boy looked up at the sky, smiled, and raised his icecream cone as high as his arm would reach. It showed me that that was the way to take life. Perhaps that's the way for you to take the church.

As ever,   Dom

Dear X,

Your letter in answer to my last one has pleased me a lot. I was afraid you might be shocked at reading my reflections on death. Few among my friends can understand how a well-meaning and outwardly cheerful person like myself can be so powerfully drawn to non-existence. I don't altogether understand it myself but I know it is sincere. In this connection I might add that 'to understand all is to cure all' seems to me most complete nonsense. Vastly more is understood today about the workings of the human psyche than was known a hundred years ago and how many neurotics can claim to have been cured? Understanding, even considered as one of the Holy Spirit's great blessings, is not an infallible specific against uncharity. One of the advantages of this correspondence of ours, so it seems to me, is that we are coming more and more to understand one another's point of view, and to this extent it is being helpful to both of us, but it has not *cured* anything. All a correspondence can do is to air opinions, dubious or downright erroneous, which need to be cured. The actual work of correction has to be a mixture of grace and consent. That is why I think endurance is more important than feeling; endurance of any trial you care to mention gives the feelings time to change. Loneliness can be accepted, doubt can be gradually replaced by at least some sort of conviction, despair can be so calmed down by endurance as eventually to elicit hope. Even the backward-looking miseries such as shame, remorse, guilt and the sense of failure can be endured in a spirit of humility and looked upon as part of the debt which all of us have to pay.

So when you write about 'irresistible impulses' I

still wonder how far the impulses really are irresistible. I know mine are not. Don't you think that if you gave yourself time to check the impulse you would find it was only an instinct? Instincts are always trying to get out of control and the best way for them to do this is to persuade the rational part of us that the will can no longer function here. That nature must be appeased is a fallacy. Obviously nature must be allowed to express itself, but not at all cost. If the natural could at any time claim the right to outweigh the supernatural then there would be no point in faith or obedience or religion. You know this as well as I do, but what I think you do not see clearly enough is the difference between the natural impulse and the supernatural cause of the impulse. You tend to isolate the compulsion, separating temptation from trial. Think more of impulses as trials of faith (or hope or charity) and not so much as imperative urges to which resistance is impossible. Here is a quotation from the Book of Sirach (which in my day used to be called Ecclesiasticus but let it pass), chapter two: 'When you come to serve the Lord, prepare yourself for trials. Be sincere of heart and steadfast, undisturbed in time of adversity . . . accept whatever befalls you and in crushing misfortune be patient . . . turn not away lest you fall . . . woe to the sinner who treads a double path . . . woe to you who have lost hope; what will you do at the visitation of the Lord?' Read the whole chapter, the key words you will recognise at a glance. You will see how 'irresistible impulse', 'natural compulsion', 'situation ethic' are terms which do not even touch the main issue. They excuse nothing. All they do is to try to explain everything. Anyway read that chapter. It can be part of your Lenten exercise.

Happy Ash Wednesday,

Dom

LETTER 34

Dear X,

You don't mention my last letter so we can now drop the subject of death which I felt was beginning to bore. Instead you ask about Lent. Today being Ash Wednesday, and the mails being what they are, you will not get what follows until halfway through the penitential season. Lent has been so played down by the church—unfortunately as I think—that one has to invent all sorts of substituting horrors of one's own. The mistake is to think that the list of things 'given up for Lent' is the important part. Any fool can be hungry. And there are other good reasons apart from Lent to give up smoking and drinking. My advice would be to look to the positive rather than to the negative aspect of Lent: more prayer, more reading, the stations of the cross, the rosary said *slowly* . . . rather than putting a ban on television or newspapers. This may strike you as very old-fashioned but this year I am taking the 'seven words from the cross' and seeing how they can be worked into both my own life and the contemporary scene. Look them up: three of our Lord's last recorded sayings are about others and four are about himself. I have never applied this technique before and already I am finding it helpful. I'm not suggesting that the whole of your prayer time should be devoted to working out the application, whom the words were addressed to, how literally they are to be taken, because this would be too much an intellectual exercise and consequently a distraction, but when not at your usual set time for prayer the 'words' can be pondered. The final three hours of our Lord's life must in any case be extremely significant to the christian, so what he said during them deserves to be seriously examined and taken to heart.

Considering what a lot was said by the prophets on the subject of repentance it is astonishing how little its place in spirituality and religion is understood today. Having said above that the positive rather than the negative element of penance is to be looked at it may sound odd that I should immediately cite the theme, the invariable theme, of the prophets. So before I go any further I must insist that repentance is positive. 'Conversion from' supposes 'conversion to'. Jesus preached repentance as emphatically as his cousin St John the Baptist did, and the doctrine of Jesus was nothing if not positive and constructive. John had his head chopped off, Jesus was crucified: both demanded a return to the Lord. In our soft, candy-coated, gift-wrapped, air-conditioned, hot-waterbottled age we tend to forget that the hopes held out for the good christian throw black shadows for the bad one, and though mortification is not the first purpose of Lent the very act of stretching out to the resurrection has to be a straining to get away from the magnetic pull of the world which is pointing in the opposite direction.

Personally I always find it easier to make suggestions about prayer than about penance. Penance can be taken up in a spirit which has little or nothing to do with love, and unless penance is prayerful as well as penitential—that is to say orientated towards Christ's passion and not purely punitive—I doubt if our Lent can mean much. That's why I recommend the consideration of our Lord's words from the cross. All seven of them are about love.

In union with your attempt,

Dom

Dear X,

Your troubles are mounting I'm afraid. This does not surprise me because it invariably happens to people who give themselves to God as you have manifestly done. But they must not be allowed to get out of proportion to the rest of your life. Stress is not a bad thing in the spiritual life: it can prevent laziness and lead to putting all your confidence in God. But overstress is bad. Beyond a certain point—a point which neither you nor anyone else can determine with certainty—tension makes for compensatory measures. This means nerves, and spiritual as well as psychological imbalance. When the mind is overburdened it breaks out in one of two ways. It either grasps at life or else tries to destroy it. It can do this almost simultaneously. Greed and aggression pitted against despair and destruction. The threshold of endurance, which is what we were discussing in an earlier exchange of letters, is different in all of us. Each of us has to judge just how much he can put up with. Tolerance of other people is not half as tricky to handle as tolerance of oneself reacting to certain pressures. Disappointments discovered in oneself or others, failure to realise what seemed a clearcut duty or even a God-given vocation, shock at coming across a scandal or a betrayal: these are things which can go beyond the limit of a goodwill acceptance. 'Even the toughest and strongest among us' wrote John Cowper Powys, 'may be sent howling to a suicidal collapse.' I wish there were someone closer to you than I am, someone you could go to see when the loneliness was getting beyond you, who would know how to deal with the howling and prevent the collapse. Merely changing the environment geographically would not help much, but steam has to be let off somehow or the explosion is inevitable. Self-punishing people who are at the same time perfectionists have a particularly hard time and need to be listened to. I am not a good listener and am at the disadvantage of not being near at hand, so you will have to find someone who can prevent you from feeling hemmed in by life, especially by the spiritual life. To be avoided at all cost is the sense, which I seem to see as being on the increase, of having been trapped into misery as the result of your conversion. I don't say this is feeling sorry for yourself in the accepted meaning of the term, but I do say that feeling smothered by a whole lot of interior and exterior cares is a danger. It could induce a violent reaction against religion. Don't let this idea become an added worry but remember that the threat is there if you do nothing about it. And if you are sensible I think you can do a lot about it. Could you not get hold of a priest who is about your own age and tell him some of the things you have told me? I am too old as well as too far away. The right kind of layman would do. Someone who is on the spot and who understands. (In my last letter I said what nonsense it was to claim that to understand all is to cure all. This is different. You don't need a cure; you need direction. Also you need friendship.)

Confidently always,
Dom

Dear X,

This letter may turn out to be rather brutal, but if so it will only be because I am attacking myself for the same things that make me uneasy about you. We are very much alike: far too introverted, questioning, ready to give up. We both need to be defused. There's too much building up inside us, and since we have both found that being in the right place is not the solution we must somehow fashion a place within ourselves which at least enables us to see where the solution lies even if it does not altogether guarantee it. The chief difference between you and me is that you are always thinking that the turmoil will one day stop, whereas I, having lived much longer, know that the turmoil goes on until the last day of life. Not the same turmoil, objectively, but struggle of some sort. It's just the shape that alters, the object of conflict, but the tension is there all the time and one simply has to wait and hope. The mistake you make is to think you can shoot down adversity and cover the area more or less in your stride. The mistake I make is not to shoot enough, not to stride. The trouble with most of us today, growing up in front of the looking glass, is self-concern. This is a nice way of describing narcissism. If we cannot help being egocentric at least we should try to balance it with the effort to focus attention on what can be done to alleviate the difficulties of other people. The more we can concern ourselves with the physical, mental, spiritual, material affairs of our friends, or even of complete strangers, the less we shall bother with our own reflections. I have a feeling that the love affair which caused you so much suffering and heart-searching some time ago would have settled itself sooner and more painlessly if you had been more humble about it and seen it for what it was. How she regarded it I do not of course know, but from the way you described it in your letters I had the impression that you were more worried about its effect upon you than about what it might be doing for her. Self-concern, narcissism, is at the back of most broken marriages. It is probably at the back of broken religious vows and of defections from the priesthood. What it amounts to is the projection of self rather than the search for the essential thing. The essential thing is always love, whether thought of in the context of divine or human love, and there is a tendency in all of us to dramatise ourselves in relation to it. The effect love should have is to make us forget ourselves, but unfortunately it more often has the opposite effect. We look into what we think is the depths of the pool and are satisfied to gaze at our own reflections on the surface.

From self-absorption it is only a step to self-canonisation, self-deification. I have known priests, and I am sure you have known married men, who believe themselves to be infallible, beyond criticism, not to be questioned on any point at all. The tendency can grow. It can destroy a man's judgment, let alone his compassion and understanding. The odd thing is that often it can originate in a basic insecurity. Hesitant and unsure of himself, a man can begin to shore up what little self-esteem he possesses until he ends up by being all self-esteem and there is very little room for the virtues which you and I are trying to cultivate. Prayer? Humility? Thoughtfulness? He knows all about them and if anyone doubts him he becomes either arrogant or touchy. Now don't look round at other people for illustrations of this. Try yourself out on it, and I will try the same on myself.

As ever, and I hope not arrogantly,   Dom

Dear X,

Listen, you idiot, the grace of faith is like a blood transfusion. You were weak before with loss of blood, and now you have in you the strength of faith. Whether you like it or not the grace is there. It may condemn you or it may free you, but you cannot get away from it. Some people (I am one of them) are imprisoned from the start. I cannot escape God. I knew God before I knew anything else. But you are different: you have discovered God. It comes to the same in the end, I suppose, because life for people like us is meaningless without God. But from the practical point of view there has to be co-operation. Not even a blood transfusion would be any good if the person to whom it was given were dead. Months ago I was writing to you about how love was really one and how human love took its colour from divine love. The principle is the same: the transfusion of the infinite to the finite, the absolute to the relative, the eternal to the temporal. Whether your problem of the moment is faith or love, you do complicate so. The solution is to unify not to divide.

You remember what I was trying to say in my last letter: how that true spirituality was to be found in simplicity and not in multiplicity. By one of those strokes of coincidence (which I prefer to attribute to the Holy Spirit and not to chance) I read this morning that in his catholic days Tertullian wrote: 'After Christ we have no cause for further curiosity, and after the gospel no need of further searching. Once we believe we have nothing else to believe. The first article of our faith is that there is nothing else to which faith need be applied'. We baptised christians have faith. It is in us as our tonsils are in us. We can suppress our faith but we cannot get rid of it as we can get rid of our tonsils. If only people could be persuaded that Christ is the pleroma, the alpha and omega, the fullness of God, the all in all, there would be nothing more to worry about. Grace tells us this but we don't listen. Love flows out from Christ and we shut ourselves off from the flow. Life is given us for the express purpose of finding God and uniting ourselves with him, and we avoid developing the essence of life by fooling about with the accidentals of life. God knows I do this as much as anyone. More than most people do. I try to avoid life altogether. But at least this has taught me to tell other people not to make the same mistake.

It would be much easier, as far as that goes, not to believe in God at all, not to get caught up in human love, not to have to think about anything but self-preservation. But it is not a question of what would be easier but what in fact is. Since we cannot ignore our souls, and what our souls show us about grace, we are stuck with faith. We are stuck not only with faith but with the church and the existing situation. In fact we are quite simply stuck. This is not fatalism, it is faith. There is all the difference between the two. Fate supposes determinism, faith supposes grace. And grace supposes free will. But that's about enough for today. Anyway it has given me a splitting headache, so the next move must come from you.

As always,
Dom

Dear X,

I am wondering whether a lot of your troubles wouldn't be made more bearable by really hard work. Like all artists you work at a ferocious pace when there is something you want to do, and you put your whole self into it. This is a good thing: it prevents you from thinking about yourself. You also get a good deal of satisfaction from the thought that you are a hard worker. But are you? What I think of as hard work is disciplined work, regular work, starting when you are supposed to and knocking off when you are supposed to. It may be drudgery-work or excitement-work; it may be physical or intellectual; it may mean digging or writing poetry. (My own suggestion would be manual work: the soil is therapy in a way which the notebook and the typewriter are not.) I am speaking from experience here. Throughout my adult life I think I have welcomed the prospect of hard work. This goes for digging, carving stone, writing books and preaching retreats. Even painting, which most people seem to think of as a polite hobby. Not that I have liked starting work—almost always I have dreaded it—but I have known instinctively that I would be more at peace inside when flogging myself to work than when allowing myself time off. The particular brand of occupation doesn't matter much. What matters is the perseverance; even the timetable matters. Perhaps this is an attitude of mind which I inherited from my father, who was extremely exact and conscientiously regular, but it is also something I have had to cultivate because I am by nature lazy. I am also, like you, impulsive and reluctant to commit myself. I am sure you hate accepting orders for a particular work, and deadlines, and being given instructions and conditions as to how the work must be done. But this is all part of it, and the tension it creates is not as restrictive as it seems. On the contrary it is liberative. It frees you from the indulgence of doing everything in your own way and at your own pace. The artistic gift is not meant to be a luxury; it can be sheer hell. But to assume that it can be absolved from the responsibility of order and discipline can involve you in far more trouble in the long run. The creative artist is not given a free pass to independence: he is a labourer like any other. Labourers have to clock in, take orders, work on until the hooter goes. This side of your life has been neglected, and I think if you gave it more attention you would be less inclined to question everything, feel so inadequate, give in to moods of loneliness and despair.

This is a shorter letter than usual. My letters have been getting too long and too boring. I sometimes suspect you don't read them. You are probably daunted by the prospect of having to read page after page. So you can expect a more crisp and constricted reply in future.

As always,
Dom

Dear X,

All right: you can't work steadily in the way I outlined, and the reason you give is that you are not settled. You don't have a routine job, you are not rooted to any particular place, you don't belong anywhere, you are not committed to anything or anyone, your future is not a reality to you and you have no ambitions. I grant you all this but I still think that if you are to overcome your religious and psychological obstacles you have got to anchor yourself somewhere or in something. It is not primarily a question of place—though this would help enormously—but a question of habit. It is a question of finding yourself, what you are meant to be. There are some people who take on a way of life and never give another thought to possible alternatives. They are the lucky ones. It is largely a matter of temperament. But it is also a matter of grace. Stability is a gift from God before it is an inborn quality. You do not have this gift, and nor do I. In neither of us is it an inborn quality. But it is something to be looked for and prayed for if the best is to be got out of us for the glory of God. Unless we belong we cannot pray properly, work properly, love properly. Unless we strike roots we are in a state of flux. This means that we are at the mercy of the next mood that comes along, the next enthusiasm, the next temptation to desert. The trouble about you is that you are never at home anywhere. One has to be at home somewhere or one is a foreigner everywhere. It is no fun being an exile. Don't come to think of yourself as a misplaced person or you will never be able to live the interior life. Aliens never really accept. Try to settle. For years you have been bivouacking on an idealised rooftop but to bivouac at all is a mistake. Whether it is a rooftop in the sky or a carpark on the ground makes no difference. The difference is whether one adjusts and accepts or rejects and rebels.

As ever,
Dom

LETTER 40

Dear X,

Your reply to my last letter showed more self-knowledge than I thought you possessed. To despise oneself is better than to congratulate oneself. What you said at the end—'you talk about the necessity of settling but I notice you have been on the move for years, now in one monastery now in another, now in one job now in another, so the advice would have been more convincing if it had come from someone who had stuck to the same place and to the same work'—is perfectly true. But perhaps because of my changes and uprootings I can sympathise with those who find it hard to settle. Anyway the charge of restlessness gives me an excuse, once again, to say a bit more about myself. (And this of course is always an agreeable occupation.)

From my early childhood—and I can remember the occasion which first brought it home to me—I have known that I was by nature a nomad. In Alexandria at the age of about six I felt an affinity with the *beduin* who used to ride in from the desert past our house and who seemed to me the symbols of high romance. Though in a vague sort of way I knew I would never belong anywhere, I knew too that to run from belonging would be wrong. To be a wanderer was one thing; to be a deserter was another. If I was doomed to be forever restless and not to settle—'footloose' is the term—I was not doomed to betray. As I grew older I looked for something which would tie me down, which would defend me against my roving, so the vows of religion came to have an attraction for me. But one should not approach monasticism as an insurance policy. Fortunately for me my superiors have accepted my inability to settle, to belong and feel I fitted in, so have either shoved me into a series of jobs or have allowed me to find things to do which kept me more or less interested if not locally pinned down. I tell you this because I hope you will not experience the same sense of being a migrant worker, the sense of having to try to find interest in works which one knows will be only temporary. Inevitably such interest is forced and unsatisfactory, and the results are just as inevitably disappointing. But I suppose it is something to be able to show interest, if only to keep faith, so matters might be a lot worse. At my age one does not have to throw oneself into projects of one kind or another simply to prove that one is still alive, but at your age it is important to do two things: to cultivate interests and to keep on with them. Of my Benedictine vows the vow of stability is the one I find the hardest. You have taken no vows but I think you have to guard against instability. You have a wider range of talents than I have so you will find it all the more difficult to be stable. You know your tendency to switch. We have to take ourselves as God made us, whether restless or settled, but I cannot believe he made us to be dabblers. Still less to be deserters.

So much for my resolution to keep my letters short.

As always,
Dom

LETTER 41

Dear X,

Your letters always surprise me. Suddenly you seem resentful at my frankness. This is something new. Do believe me that I am frank only because I am concerned, and concerned only because I am sympathetic. I made the comparison between your situation and mine, between your temperament and mine, only because it seemed to me we are both much in the same boat. You have looked for satisfaction in art, in religion, in a love affair, in a vocation to religious life: I have looked for satisfaction in the monastic life. Both of us have been chasing dreams which have not been realised. Your ideals are out of reach and so are mine. All I have done in this correspondence is to repeat in different words that ideals are meant to be out of reach or they would not be ideals but only projects or ambitions. Now that I have given up hope of finding perfection on the monastic level, or happiness in it, I am more at peace than I have been for years. I recommend you to follow me in this. Perfection in this life does not exist. It is an infinite thing, to be found only in the next life. I doubt if happiness in this life can exist. Contentment can but not happiness —not for longer than about twenty minutes anyway. Acceptance exists, endurance exists, perseverance exists. Don't, *don't* go running after rainbows.

Last night I couldn't sleep so took a sleeping pill. It didn't work so I took another. I still could not sleep. I could not read or pray or type, so I went for a walk. It was after midnight and snowing quite hard but there was just enough moonlight to prevent me from bumping into things. I trudged through about six inches of snow and felt strangely elated. For about twenty minutes I stood looking at the mountains which, though white when seen in daylight, looked like black icebergs, dead and sad against the sky. To me the scene seemed, in my drugged state, a symbol of this human existence which I dislike so much. One treads crunching and stumbling over acres of virgin surface. But it is only surface. One sees outlines but they are only outlines. One feels cold but these are only feelings. It is the solid rock that counts, the primeval stuff. The snow will melt, the cold will give way to heat, we shall die. But the mountains which look so black and hostile will see dawn after dawn, sunshine and warmth. What seems black in one's life will turn out not to be so black after all. I thought of you and how darkness is never meant to last for ever. But now, in the broad light of day, the significance of all this seems to have evaporated and is no help at all. The only conclusion I can draw from this night-time ramble (as from experience and life itself) is that the soul in prayer must not expect help except from God himself. Only he is substantial, everything else is an arrangement of stage props. Symbols must be accepted as symbols. Once we start thinking of symbols as being more important than the things they symbolise we are in a world of unreality, we are in Disneyland. The only thing that matters is the love of God, and to come to this we must pray. Walking about in a romantic setting does no good at all. To look for satisfaction or 'happiness' (whatever that means) in anything short of God is to lay oneself open to disappointment. Also to loneliness, doubt, fear and despair. Forget about happiness and satisfaction: get to work on prayer and love.

As ever,
Dom

Dear X,

I could almost have taken a bet that sooner or later
you would have a shot at pentecostalism. It is just the
sort of thing which would attract you. I am sure it has
helped a lot of people who have been in your state
and has put a lot of people on to an authentic way of
prayer. A number of bishops have backed it and
quantities of priests have joined the movement and
advised it to the faithful. But I would say that it is
something which has to be approached with caution.
Obviously the Holy Spirit can draw souls in extraordinary ways but I personally would always feel safer
in seeing a more down-to-earth means of communication. What especially bothers me is the 'gift of
tongues' which seems to impress you so much. I am all
for people of different denominations getting together for prayer, particularly for silent prayer, but
I am a bit suspicious of flamboyant demonstrations of
devotion. St Paul allowed for the faithful co-operating
with the gift of tongues, and it has at times been accepted as a valid sign of authentic prayer, but St Paul
if you notice is not keen. He does not take it to be a
sign of orthodoxy. In fact he seems to be rather against
the whole thing. Look up 1 Corinthians, chapter 14,
where he says: 'Just suppose I should come to you
speaking in tongues. What good will I do if my speech
does not have some revelation or prophecy or instruction for you? If you do not utter intelligible speech
because you are speaking in tongues how will anyone
know what you are saying? You will be talking to the
air . . . Since you have set your ear on spiritual gifts,
try to be rich in those that build up the church. This
means that the man who speaks in a tongue should

pray for the gift of interpretation. If I pray in a tongue my spirit is at prayer but my mind contributes nothing . . . how will the one who does not comprehend be able to say "Amen" to your thanksgiving? He will not know what you are saying. You will be uttering praise very well indeed but the other man will not be helped. I would rather speak five words which were intelligible to instruct others than ten thousand words in a tongue'. About charismatic gifts, which are now so popular, it would be worth your while to look up Col 2 : 8; 2 Thess 2 : 15; 1 Tim 1 : 3-9; 2 Tim 3 : 1-5; 2 Tim 4 : 3; and 2 Cor 11 : 3,4. If you do not understand the Holy Spirit's way of working—and you can understand this only by accepting the church's ruling —you are in grave danger of exposing yourself to subjectivism, emotionalism, illuminism. If Ronald Knox had lived I am sure he would have had a lot to say in his *Enthusiasm* about the neo-pentecostalism which is sweeping Europe and America. For my part I am less concerned about transcendental meditation and the Jesus freaks than I am about this pseudo-communication with the third person of the Trinity. Also it is worth noting that Plutarch in the fourth century describes precisely the same phenomena manifesting themselves in the pagan mystic cults of his time. The gift of tongues is by no means a christian monopoly. There is a good deal more I could say on this subject but I do not want to turn you against what may be a genuine call from the Holy Spirit. You can judge only by its effects, and if pentecostalism is bringing you closer to God I would be the last person to get in the way with clumsy criticism. Tell me more.

As ever in Christ's genuine Spirit,

Dom

Dear X,

I was not at all surprised at the way you felt about my letter on the subject of pentecostalism. I can only tell you how its effects have struck *me*. Some of the effects have struck me as singularly unfortunate. I know a good case can be made for what it has done in bringing souls to our Lord but so far as I am concerned the more vociferous members of the cult—and it is a cult, not an expression of catholic spirituality blessed by the Pope (who seems highly suspicious of its emotional and illuminist manifestations)—show only the side of it which by-passes authority, the sacramental system, and our Lady. Any elitist group which claims to be in closer communication with the Holy Spirit than the rosary-saying, stations-making, mass-going, frequently-confessing catholic faithful will not get much favour from me. You, with your impulsive enthusiasms, are a sitting duck to movements which take pot shots at peasant piety. I, with my cradle catholic upbringing, am on the side of the peasant. You tell me that many of our old-fashioned catholic practices smack of superstition—indulgences, the use of holy water, the blessing of medals, the importance attached to relics, the invocation of St Antony when things can't be found, the application of St Walburga's oil, the special quality of Lourdes water and so on—but isn't there just as much superstition in believing that the elect have a hot line to the Holy Ghost and that this being so there is no need to call upon our Lady and the saints, no need to visit the blessed sacrament, no need to confess to a priest so long as one is genuinely sorry for one's sins? The only pentecostalists whom I have met have seemed to me to be a bit short on humility—ready enough to enlarge upon what the Holy Spirit has done to them and how they have advanced under the influence of this charismatic grace but not awfully objective as to the Holy Spirit's work in the world and in the church—so I have naturally shied away from them. But I am quite ready to believe that there is a side of the question which you have seen and which I have not. Anyway that's what I think, and I am perfectly ready to bow in my opinion to higher authority.

As ever in our joint obedience to the church,

Dom

Dear X,

In answering your letters I have always to guard against prejudice. You have a way of stirring in me the acids of controversy. Our correspondence is meant to be conducted on a spiritual and not a propaganda level. When in your last letter you said that anything which drew souls to an appreciation of spiritual reality was worth trying I felt like getting you on the longdistance telephone and telling you how wrong you were. Have you read Huxley's *Doors of Perception*? That book had a lot to say about appreciation of spiritual reality but it advocated a certain drug for its realisation. Surely you would not say that in the recognition of truth and the vision of beauty a man should get himself high on drugs? But this is what you imply. Truth is its own proof, beauty and goodness are their own incentive. The senses are stimulated by external means, the spirit is moved by a quite different catalogue of powers. People will tell you that *Godspell* and *Jesus Christ Superstar* are bringing our Lord to millions who would never otherwise come across the gospel, and how wonderful it is that young people are attracted to the basic theme of love. But it is better not to reach our Lord at all than to reach a parody of our Lord. Jesus in football shorts jumping about the stage and screaming fabricated doctrine is not the second person of the Trinity. Where the dignity of Christ is lost sight of the divinity follows suit. It is simply not true that whatever draws attention to religion and spirituality is bound to be to the good. The devil makes use of this idea and delusion follows. If the earlier heresies claimed Jesus to be more God than man these latter heresies claim him to be more man than God. Heresy is an aspect of truth seen in isolation, and the error of our time is the rationalisation of a truth and the isolating of it.

You asked for this.   As ever,

Dom

LETTER 45

Dear X,

Let me try another approach and come up with another remedy for your religious and psychological ills. May you not be running with the wrong pack? Your friends seem mostly to be hedonists, agnostics, playboys and easy-going women. Just as funny people need funny people to mix with, and bores call out for bores, spiritual people should be able to find other spiritual people as friends. I do not mean that you must surround yourself with pious people whose conversation is about encyclicals and revelations and bishops, but that it would help to have a few men and women whom you could rely upon to have the same sort of outlook as you have. It's not enough to know a practising catholic or two: you need people who pray. I don't think you pray enough. You did pray, after your conversion, but more recently your letters have shown a certain indifference towards the strictly interior life. I think if you mixed with souls to whom prayer was the centre of their lives you would feel an affinity which you lack in your worldly relationships. You will tell me that interior souls do not lie thick on the ground, and that such as you have come across do not make the most entertaining companions, but surely you could cultivate, through your social contacts, a handful of people who know what it is to be recollected and who are searching for perfection? I am not asking you to form a group. A group always ends up with coffee and chocolate biscuits. All I am suggesting is that you go to fewer parties and avoid the more amoral of the men and women who take up such a large part of your life.

You see my letters really are getting shorter.

As ever, Dom

LETTER 46

Dear X,

My last letter, as I knew when I was writing it, would be a target for many arrows. All right then, put the thing the other way round. *You* start making prayer the centre of your life and leave the kindred spirits to gather when God decides to pull them in. Unless you have taken on the spiritual life seriously and completely you will be drawn to waste a lot of time and grace in fooling around with the wrong sort of person. After all you are fairly free and could therefore give more time to prayer, and though time is not the whole story it is a factor without which the habit of recollection cannot be built up. Prayer feeds on prayer, and when the soul is nourished spiritually you will find that your reactions become instinctively Christ-orientated. Where before, in your non-praying days, decisions depended on what suited you and how you happened to be feeling, now, if you give yourself to prayer you will make your judgments more and more according to what suits God and not according to your mood. Don't be afraid of what the prayer life may be getting you into—'lest having him I have nothing else beside'—but trust that whatever you may be getting into God will give you the grace to handle in his way. 'I live now, not I, but Christ lives in me.'

Yours,
Dom

Dear X,

The reason why I had not said more in my earlier letters about prayer and the various techniques put forward by the textbooks is that I had assumed you had been given all the standard training in the novitiate. From your letter I learn now that you have had no sort of instruction and are eager to be told how to go about praying mentally. It surprises me that you have lasted so long trying to find your own way. Most people, lacking at least some guidance and general principles, give up. Granted that only the Holy Spirit can show souls how to pray, and that no two souls learn the practice of it in the same way, there are a few elementary approaches which can be taught and which individual souls can choose from.

The necessity of learning a way to pray mentally you have already grasped or you would not be writing to me for a lesson in how to start. Before you even start in the actual exercise you should know that the first purpose of prayer is to give glory to God. Whatever good the person praying gets out of it is secondary. Prayer is not only the most worthwhile act a man can perform in his relationship with God but also it is his most effective way of helping the world and his fellow human beings. This is because prayer supposes love, and love looks to God and man—both. There are other benefits attaching to it too of course: it leads to what in the East they would call 'enlightenment', it prepares the soul for suffering and disappointment, it deepens one's insight into the scriptures, it develops the virtues of patience, humility, trust, hope, and all the sidelines of charity. By prayer a man normally comes to know the order of his duties towards God and others, the measure to be observed in practising penance, the nothingness of self, the reason for human existence, the value to be placed on human affairs, the overall pattern of history, and a hundred other things connected or not connected with religion. Certainly prayer is needed more than ever today when everything is being questioned and when authority, whether secular or sacred, is being scorned.

So, to begin at the beginning, and by way of introduction, prayer restores as far as is possible in this life the relationship enjoyed by our first parents with God and with one another. It makes for the union which was destroyed by original sin, the harmony which existed in man's individual make-up, and the integrity of his relationship with the created world in general. As soon as the imbalance took place there had to be corrective influences: prayer, faith, fidelity to law, struggle to appreciate the supernatural and to respond to the implications of the supernatural. I need hardly say that when you set yourself to pray either mentally or vocally, you do not have to bear all these factors in mind—nothing but distraction would result if you attempted it—but this is the background against which prayer is performed.

Enough for one day. In my next letter I'll try to outline what one does in prayer, or tries to do. Always given God's grace it is not nearly such a complicated activity as it is made out to be and as may appear from what has been said above.

Counting on the Holy Spirit

As ever,

Dom

LETTER 48

Dear X,

So you are on for it—this course on how to pray? Remember I'm no expert on the subject, and a poor performer when it comes to what I do during prayer, but I can at least hand on to you what the authorities say about it and make a few suggestions along the way.

Most manuals of prayer devote their opening chapters on meditation and how this form of prayer has been recommended for centuries. I feel myself that this is more of a token than an affirmation *sine qua non*. Rather in the way that a tourist owes it to his tour of Paris to visit the Louvre, the writer of the textbook dutifully repeats what he has read in earlier textbooks and what he feels his public expects from him. I wonder how many people actually practise meditation according to the rules laid down? The prayer of meditation is described as taking a scene from our Lord's life, visualising and thinking about it, applying it to one's own condition, and finally making resolutions drawn from the conclusions arrived at. In the same way the soul is encouraged to meditate upon this or that doctrine of the church, this or that virtue. Experience seems to show that this preliminary stage of prayer seldom satisfies the soul for long; it is felt to depend too much on imaginative reconstruction or theological speculation, and not upon inciting the will to praise or allowing the mind to rest quietly in God's presence. Some may be able to keep it up, but most people drop formal meditation as just described after about a month at the outside. I think I stuck it for a week.

So what do we do now, when the imagination has exhausted the possibilities of the pictured scene and the intellect has wearied of metaphysics? As soon as we find we are getting little out of this form of prayer —which only qualifies as prayer insofar as it draws the soul to worship and this may not become an attraction until almost the whole time of prayer has gone on picturing details or wondering about catechism definitions—we should firmly and without scruple pass on to making acts of the will. This really is prayer because the visual content is reduced, the speculation is suppressed, and there is the definite desire to worship. The will to praise (or express sorrow for sin, or to make acts of hope, thanksgiving, longing, acceptance and so on) is the beginning of what the books call discursive prayer. (But forget about the terms.) You talk to God and are not merely concerned in talking about him to yourself. When your own spontaneous acts of the will begin to flag, you draw upon the psalms or any other part of the scriptures which appeal to you, and repeat them to God as reflecting your own mood or need. This is the prayer of 'forced acts', and for most people it continues for a quite considerable time. Gradually the 'acts' become less forced and are repeated at longer intervals. Also they tend to become 'affections'—that is to say they become more loving—and more personal, intimate, incommunicable as far as other people are concerned. The prayer is slowed down and the soul is conscious of wanting to say very little and instead to feel the attraction of being receptive rather than active. The fewer expressions the better, the simpler the wording the better. The time of prayer is spent in wanting God and his will. But I shall have more to say about what is called the prayer of simple regard in my next letter.

I hope you have started practising some of this,

as ever, Dom

LETTER 49

Dear X,

I left off if you remember with a mention of the prayer of simple regard. Now though this, like every other prayer, is elicited by grace, there is nothing strictly supernatural about it. Not, anyway, in its early stages. It is a state to which most souls arrive who have been faithful in producing their forced acts, their God-orientated affections and aspirations, and who have tried to develop the habit of recollection outside prayer time. I would imagine that all souls who have seriously committed themselves to the interior life feel this longing to communicate without words or with as few words as possible. For them the psalmist's words 'Be still and know that I am God' (or 'be still and *see* that I am God' as in some renderings) probably sums up their prayer for them. Some are kept back from launching out into such a silent prayer from a fear that they may be giving in to laziness, from a fear that they may be laying themselves open to the error of quietism, from the fear of moving into a higher form of prayer before God had made them ready for it. But if they honestly feel more at home in such a prayer than in the busy prayer which they have been practising up to now, and if they cannot pray with the senses any longer, and if they are not looking for 'illuminations and revelations' which would make them superior to other souls, then they not only may but should advance to the simple act of waiting upon God. They may have to return to a more discursive prayer for a time if their new-found simple regard fills up with distractions. But simplicity of worship is, nevertheless, a stage to be aimed at. Indeed it is the beginning of contemplation.

Now the distinction is drawn between 'acquired' and 'infused' contemplation. If I were you I would give this wrangle a miss. What can it matter what label is attached to the prayer of simplicity? In any case the term 'prayer of simplicity' is variously understood by various saints. Leave all that to the experts, to the professionals, to the jugglers in semantics. Pray as simply as you can and leave it to God to decide which category you belong to. Your object should be to remain in God's presence for as long as you can during prayer, stretching out to him, accepting whatever kind of prayer he sends, using words when you feel like using words and not when you don't. After all the presence of God should be the natural element of the soul in the way that the air is the natural element of the bird, and the water is the natural element of the fish : it should not be too difficult for your soul, given the grace for it, to remain for quite a time in God's presence without having to stir up the emotions in an effort to keep you there. Words and emotions, beyond a certain point, can be distractions rather than expressions of praise. Often we rattle off words and whip up emotions more to satisfy ourselves that something is going on, that we are busy at work praying our heads off, than to please God. The silence of faith can be a greater tribute to God than noisy industry.

If you want to hear more about prayer, ask and I'll do my best.

Confidently yours,
Dom

LETTER 50

Dear X,

I respect your argument of course—namely 'how can you expect me, after the kind of life I have led, and the kind of world I'm forced by circumstances to work in, to practise contemplative prayer?'—and would be rather suspicious if you reacted in the opposite way, thinking you could jump straight into it and would be master of it in no time. But don't forget Mary Magdalen, who, after Christ's mother, is the classic contemplative, lived a life which was not much different from yours before she came under Jesus's influence. I think people often mistake the meaning of the term 'contemplation'. It doesn't assume the ability to contemplate what you can see but to search for what you cannot see. We are too inclined to think of contemplatives *beholding*, when we should rather think of them as directing their gaze to God who matters to them supremely but whom they are quite content not to see at all in this life. It's a perspective rather than a vision. To cite Mary Magdalen again, her experience in the garden after the resurrection of Jesus was first important because she was looking for him and only secondarily because she was granted to recognise him. I imagine that to true contemplatives God's absence is as real as his presence, and that certainly they spend longer groping for him in the dark than gazing at him in the light.

But you know when all this has been said—and there is a lot more that could be said about the stages of prayer, the divisions and subdivisions of prayer, the different schools of prayer, the systems which claim to guarantee prayer—prayer is such a person-to-person activity that in the end each of us has to evolve his own technique. I'm sure when we get to heaven we shall find that each soul has had to find his own way to God. Oh yes, we knew that Christ is the way, and that no man comes to the father but by him. But even when securely on that way—and can we be so sure of ourselves as to know that for the rest of our lives his is the only way for us and that we have no more insecurities to fear—there are nevertheless by-ways which have to be considered. There are fourlane highways all in the same direction, going all the same way, but which lane am I in? Each man has his own way of packing a suitcase, his own way of shaving, his own way of growing mushrooms. So each soul must learn, by trial and error, his own way of praying. He may never find a very sure way but so long as he is found looking, he will not be out of pocket spiritually.

Praying for you in your search,

as always,

Dom

Dear X,

You tell me that the attraction is there for the silent prayer of waiting upon God, but that when you try it either nothing happens or you are invaded by distractions. Well, what would you expect? So long as the attraction isn't invaded by doubts and a desire to go back to a more talkative prayer the thing to do is to follow it and not be discouraged by the fact that nothing seems to happen or that distractions seem to spoil the whole thing. The reason why nothing seems to happen is that God has taken over the control of your prayer and is not letting you see what he is doing. If you were to see his work you would want to interfere with it. You would think you knew better. So of course he has to work secretly. Look at it from his point of view. His object is twofold: first to keep you there, trying to pray in spite of what is apparently a waste of time, particularly when you are leaving yourself apparently wide open to distractions; secondly to transfer the whole undertaking from the natural to the supernatural. This second purpose could not be achieved if you were able to follow the process. So what God does is to freeze your mind and operate at a level which you cannot appreciate. At the surface level he allows distractions to bother you but in fact they are only 'bothering' you and are doing you no harm. Distractions are harmful only when they are deliberately followed up. (I'm sure I must have told you this before, and in any case you must have read it in a dozen books.)

If after giving this kind of simple prayer a chance for a quite considerable time, you still find you cannot manage to be at peace in it, then it might be as well to practise the Jesus Prayer for a bit—repeating over and over again 'Lord Jesus, Son of God, have mercy on my soul'—or just breathing out the Holy Name to show that you are wanting to pray and refusing to go to sleep. The whole point of the prayer of faith (which this simple-regard prayer obviously is) is persevering in a knowledge which you do not understand and a love which you do not feel. The title of one of the best books ever written about prayer should teach you this: *The Cloud of Unknowing*. Conviction has to take the place of devotion. A man standing at the foot of Snowdon knows there must be a summit to the mountain but he does not see it because it is shrouded in mist. He acts on the fact when he starts climbing. He may feel tired even in the foothills, he may feel cold as he gets nearer to the top, he will be wrapped in mist for most of the time, but what matters is that he goes on up. His purpose is weakened if he is constantly turning round and looking back. He will be tempted to try a smaller mountain or choose a route which will take him by car almost to the top. But if he is a climber and wants to do the thing in style he plods along in an upward direction and refuses alternative options. Try reading *The Cloud*. Also *The Scale of Perfection* and Dame Julian's *Revelations of Divine Love*. When you have read those, come back for more.

Continuez, Continuez—as Belloc makes God the Father say after inspecting the affairs of earth—

Dom

Dear X,

As soon as I had recommended those three books in my last letter and told you to come back for more, I felt I had made a mistake. Recommending books to people is like recommending wines: one's own taste seldom satisfies anyone else's. St Benedict at the end of the Holy Rule urged his monks to read St Basil and the Fathers. I doubt if many monks today read St Basil and the Fathers. I myself enjoy Cassian but each year when I read his two books during Lent I find myself skipping more and more. Among the moderns I think you should try Thomas Merton, especially *Seeds of Contemplation* which can be made into preparation for prayer and can even provide material for prayer. Teilhard de Chardin's *Milieu Divin* is pretty stiff but is good for exploding wrong ideas about prayer. The books that have helped me over the years of my religious life are *The Way of the Pilgrim* and Brother Lawrence's *Practice of the Presence of God*. The great thing about spiritual reading is to relate it to prayer, and if a particular book does not help you to pray give it up. It is a mistake to imagine that you have to treat spiritual reading as a penance, and that a book once started has to be read right through. This only induces disgust. Another mistake is to say to yourself 'This book helped me enormously ten years ago, so it is sure to have the same effect again'. It needn't. You have advanced in ten years and your tastes as well as your needs have changed. Read the new testament, bits of the old testament (especially Job and the psalms) which are what St Benedict calls *medicamina* or *medicamenta*: that is to say they are therapy, healing at whatever stage of our spiritual lives we read them. Our reading should be, in the actual exercise, whether we choose scriptural material or accredited works on the interior life, meditative. I mean we should not rush through one book in order to start a new one. We should make a point of stopping when we come to a point which especially strikes us, thinking it out, and if necessary going back and reading it again. In this way it becomes a sort of drawn-out prayer. It should not take the place of set times of prayer, nor should set times of prayer be spent in reading passages which have struck us outside the time of prayer, but we should realise that prayer and spiritual reading are closely connected. I suppose it would be possible to keep up a life of prayer without the help of reading—as for instance blind people would have to do—but in the ordinary way our prayer life needs the nourishment of our reading life.

Where it is a question of time—the choice between reading a spiritual book or devoting half an hour to mental prayer—prayer has first claim. This is not only because of the two prayer is more directly uniting us with God, but also because reading is as a rule connected with a subject, a particular aspect of the spiritual life, whereas prayer is directed immediately with the object, namely God. Neither reading nor study can be a substitute for prayer. Prayer, rightly ordered, is love, and there is no substitute for love. It is a temptation to preachers to dispense themselves from prayer because they have to prepare and deliver sermons. But unless the sermon comes from prayer and love there is no point in preaching it. But this is more my problem than yours.

Let me know if I can help
as ever,
Dom

LETTER 53

Dear X,

You seem to be getting interested in the whole subject of prayer. This is excellent. But be careful not to become dilettante about it, taking it up almost as an art form. Prayer is tough, and meant to be. It is a matter of faith, and faith is always hard work. Not only is it hard work but is also felt to be a most unrewarding work. This is the whole point of it. 'Blessed is he who has not seen but has believed.' The kind of prayer which I imagine you to be in at the moment is the prayer of faith. And the prayer of faith (to adapt a well-known saying) is a question of looking in a dark room for a black hat which won't fit even if you happen to find it.

What I am going to say now is not something to be remembered in prayer—the less you remember the stages in the progression of prayer the better—but is something which may show you the way in which prayer moves along from its initiation to contemplative, illuminative, and unitive prayer. At first the soul normally relies on words and images. The senses play an important part here. The lips pronounce words which are read out of books and the senses try to work up the corresponding emotions. The words are really more the author's way of addressing God. His way but not necessarily yours. This prayer is good enough as far as it goes but unless it happens to match what you happen to need or to feel, it is hardly more than a cut-out pattern for you to copy. The words are the material content, to be made use of by you just as far as they are felt to coincide with what is in your own heart and mind. Next there is the mixture of words and thought: the rosary, the stations of the cross, the

118

set exercises in the meditation books. The content here is still largely material, because the soul is relying on the senses to represent images, but a more spiritual and intellectual element has now entered in. When this kind of prayer is felt to be kaleidoscopic—the senses doing part of the work but not with any satisfaction to the soul—then the thing to do is to leave the senses out of it and concentrate on the simple thought of God. From here onwards the principal aim is simplicity and unity.

God is, in the theological sense, simple. We are (in every sense) complicated. 'For the union of two' says St Bernard, 'the elements must correspond.' You can judge this by the way in which the devil produces complication and *angst*, while God prompts to confidence and unexamining perseverance. Whether you happen to be aware of being in God's presence and love during the whole time that you are praying doesn't matter as much as *wanting* to be in his presence and love. Desire is always the important qualification. 'God does not ask for a perfect work'—the best thing St Catherine of Siena ever said, this—'but for infinite desire'. So whatever encourages the desire is the means to use. For a time it may be one book, for a time it may be another. For a time it may be nature, for a time it may be art. But these things are only means. The desire must be deliberately trained towards God and not towards the means. Your desire draws you to where your treasure is. The only treasure is God.

I hope this makes sense

as ever,

Dom

LETTER 54

Dear X,

I was half expecting you to answer as you did. You say you feel 'safer' clutching your book of devotions. Of course you do. But prayer hasn't been invented to make you feel safer. The object of prayer is to give glory to God. 'Launch out into the deep' is not a recommendation to play safe. Faith is a risk. Trust is a risk. If God is calling you to a simpler and purer form of prayer—which you have admitted in an earlier letter that he seems to be—aren't you being a little rude to him when you say 'Thanks, but at least I'll know that I'm doing something if I rattle off vocal prayers . . . whereas if I stop reading and talking what guarantee have I got that any sort of prayer is going on at all?' We shouldn't ask for guarantees. Prayer is doing without the security of guarantees: it is trust, it is a series of acts of faith. Love expresses itself in this way, and if prayer means anything at all it means love.

Someone ought to write a story about a man who found a prayerbook in an attic which suited his every aspiration. He was enchanted by it, and every time he went to church he took it with him and it worked like a charm. Then the time came when, knowing it by heart, it meant nothing to him. But he kept remembering that day when he found it in the attic and how holy he felt and what resolutions he made then and there to keep it always within reach as though it were a talisman. So although it was failing him now he refused to let it go. God wanted him to drop the old prayerbook and launch out into the deep but the poor man was too timid. And from being too timid he became too obstinate, and from being too obstinate he rejected all the graces God was sending him and preferred to go on hugging the prayerbook which was now not the slightest good to him. And in the end he preferred the book to God. A parallel to this depressing story might be seen in Maupassant's *Elixir du Père Gaucher,* where the monk is destroyed by the wine which it has been his good fortune to concoct. He found the recipe which was such a success at first, but in the end it was the recipe which damned him as a drunkard. But in case it wasn't Maupassant who wrote the story, and in case the monk's name was not Gaucher, let me cite other instances of the same thing. Perillos of Athens designed a bronze bull into whose hollow inside criminals were to be locked and roasted at the will of his master Phalaris. Perillos was the first frizzled victim. Morton, the inventor of the guillotine, was beheaded by his own masterpiece. Thomas Montacute, fourth earl of Salisbury, was the first to use the cannon. He was also the first Englishman to be killed by a cannon ball. Aubriot, Prefect of Paris, built the Bastille and ended up as its first prisoner. So think twice about finding a sure-fire method of prayer in case it turns round when its usefulness has been outlasted and fires you.

Pray for me,
Dom

Dear X,

Why don't we just forget about the techniques of prayer and leave the whole thing to God? All that has to be done is to stay as long as you can in God's presence and when you find you are losing contact—which happens after about a minute—make yourself aware of the fact that God's presence is all round you and that you can't escape it even if you want to. Once you are back in God's presence you simply stay in it and try to express love, gratitude, acceptance, and so on. Don't worry about how many acts of love, gratitude, acceptance and so on you make. The point is to be with God, not the subjects you discuss with him. The point is not the originality or the eloquence or the emotion or the intensity but the desire to be with God in a state of dependence and trust and love. Leave the way it's done to the professionals. You and I are not professionals. We are people who want to give glory to God in the simplest, most direct, most immediate way we know. We don't have to be articulate or sophisticated. We just have to be sincere, to be ourselves. This shouldn't be too difficult. Offer yourself to God, accept the prayer God sends you, don't push it or try to work up a prayer which isn't the prayer God wants out of you. Prayer isn't expertise; it's as ordinary as breathing. It's second nature.

That's all I know about it, so if you want to learn more you had better go to the professionals.

But if you get stuck write again,

Dom